Praise for
OVERCOMING SPIRITUAL VERTIGO

"When thinking about the Christian life, I often say, 'Blessed are the balanced for they shall find rest in the Lord.' Dwayne Mercer writes with clarity and with a shepherd's heart. He wants God's people to find confidence, direction, joy, purpose and rest as we walk with our Lord. I believe this book will encourage and help many."

—Dr. Daniel L. Akin
President of Southeastern Theological Seminary
Author of over sixteen books and numerous articles

"Are you dizzy from the doubts that surround you? Constantly plagued by a fear that prevents you from moving forward in faith? Dwayne helps us identify this 'spiritual vertigo,' understand how to operate in Bible-believing faith that takes God at His Word and overcome the doubts and fears that hinder our spiritual maturity. If you want to be marked as a man or woman of faith, this book is an excellent resource for your journey!"

—Michael Catt
Senior Pastor, Sherwood Church
Executive Producer, Sherwood Pictures
Producer, "Fireproof"
Winner of the International Christian Retail Show's 2013 Best
Young Adult Nonfiction for *Courageous Teens*

"Is what you see, hear, and experience in real life causing you to wrestle with your faith? Do past disappointments cause your trust in God to falter? In *Overcoming Spiritual Vertigo*, Dwayne Mercer addresses these difficult questions and offers the answer to experiencing courageous, bold faith for your future."

—Dr. Johnny Hunt
Senior Pastor, First Baptist Church Woodstock
Former President, Southern Baptist Convention

"Feel knocked off-balance? Questioning your faith? Dwayne Mercer has written a wonderful book teeming with biblical insights just for you—all grounded in real life experiences. Dwayne will help you dissect and understand what's going on when you feel like your faith doesn't make sense—or maybe doesn't even work. By the end, your heart will swell with courage to go the distance."

—Patrick Morley
Chairman and CEO of "Man in the Mirror"
Author of the eighteen-time bestseller, *Man in the Mirror*

"Does your faith seem attacked by reality? Have the trials of life knocked the wind out of your relationship with God? In *Overcoming Spiritual Vertigo*, my good friend Dwayne Mercer, a man who knows what that is like and has helped thousands navigate turbulent times, answers those tough questions about faith and doubt. This book is truly an encouraging word with substance! A must-read for anyone in need of hope."

—Jay Strack
Founder and President, Student Leadership University
Author of *Everything Worth Knowing I Learned Growing Up in Florida* and *The Three Success Secrets of Shamgar*

OVERCOMING SPIRITUAL VERTIGO

OVERCOMING SPIRITUAL VERTIGO

The Journey from Doubt to Courageous Faith

DWAYNE E. MERCER

PUBLICATIONS

Fort Washington, PA 19034

Overcoming Spiritual Vertigo
Published by CLC Publications

U.S.A.
P.O. Box 1449, Fort Washington, PA 19034

UNITED KINGDOM
CLC International (UK)
Unit 5, Glendale Avenue, Sandycroft, Flintshire, CH5 2QP

ISBN (cloth): 978-1-61958-225-5
ISBN (e-book): 978-1-61958-222-4

Unless otherwise noted, Scripture quotations are from the New American Standard Bible®, Copyright © 1960, 1962, 1963, 1968, 1971, 1972, 1973,1975, 1977, 1995 by The Lockman Foundation. Used by permission.

Scripture quotations marked ESV® are from the Holy Bible, English Standard Version®, copyright © 2001 by Crossway, a publishing ministry of Good News Publishers. Used by permission. All rights reserved.

Scripture quotations marked KJV are from the Holy Bible, King James Version, 1611.

Scripture quotations marked NLT are from the Holy Bible, New Living Translation, copyright © 1996, 2004, 2007, 2013. Used by permission of Tyndale House Publishers, Inc., Carol Stream, Illinois 60188. All rights reserved.

Scripture quotations marked NIV® are from the Holy Bible, New International Version®. Copyright © 1973, 1978, 1984, 2011 by Biblica, Inc.™ Used by permission of Zondervan. All rights reserved.

Scripture quotations marked NKJV are from the New King James Version®. Copyright © 1982 by Thomas Nelson. Used by permission. All rights reserved.

Bolded words in Scripture quotations are the emphasis of the author.

Dedication

To my six amazing grandchildren, Noah, Owen, Piper, Elspeth, Gwynn, and baby boy Mercer. May all of you live lives of courageous faith!

Contents

Acknowledgments

I wish to personally extend a special thanks to my administrative assistant, Joey Everest, whose tireless efforts and dedication helped make this book possible.

I also thank CrossLife Church for granting me sabbatical time to pen this work. The support of my church, its members and staff, prove to be a constant reinforcement in my life.

Thank you to my wonderful wife, Pam, who has steadfastly journeyed beside me through times of both spiritual vertigo and courageous faith!

Introduction

Read This First

It was the middle of a typical hot summer night at our home outside of Orlando. My wife, Pam, and our two younger children were visiting family in Georgia while our oldest son and I stayed behind. We were sound asleep after a long day of golfing in near 100-degree temperatures when I suddenly woke up in a cold sweat. The room appeared to be spinning. I tried to get up but each attempt made me feel sick to my stomach. To make matters worse, my brain felt like it was moving around inside my head and my eyes seemed to be dancing. I had lost all perspective of direction and I was scared. I thought, *Am I dying? Should I call for help?*

I tried to cry out to my son, who was sleeping in his bedroom, but my voice wouldn't carry. Every time I tried to reach for the phone, I felt like the ceiling was attacking me.

Eventually, I mustered the determination to turn, grab the phone and dial 911. By the time the paramedics arrived, I was so disoriented that they had to wake my son to unlock the front door because I couldn't move from the bed. They immediately strapped me to a gurney and whisked me away to the hospital. When I got there, the doctors administered intravenous fluids to hydrate me. They diagnosed me with a severe case of vertigo due to dehydration.

The high temperatures during our golf outing earlier that day left me exhausted by the end of the round. I'd also been drinking diet soda all day instead of water, which caused me to become extremely dehydrated. That night, I experienced vertigo because of it. The best way I can describe this condition is that your brain and eyes have a functional disconnect and your brain is unable to process what your eyes are seeing.

You may have never had physical vertigo; but I believe most of us experience "spiritual vertigo," a phrase I first heard from *New York Times* best-selling author Tim Keller, the founding pastor of Redeemer Presbyterian Church in New York City.[1] During spiritual vertigo, we become spiritually disoriented. We know what the Bible teaches, but what we see, hear or experience does not match what our faith tells us should be true.

As a result, we begin to live in a world of doubt. We know God is sovereign, loving and gracious. We hear sermons and read books about being a giant killer, a lion tamer, and more than a conqueror in Christ. However, we cannot bring ourselves to believe it. How can we have courageous faith when the everyday challenges and disappointments of life make us dizzy with doubt?

Doubt-filled faith is extremely prevalent in society today. It is estimated that only 13 percent of the millennial generation (those born between 1982 and 2002) consider any type of spirituality to be important in their lives.[2] Author John Dickerson reports that they drop out and don't return because they simply do not believe anymore.[3]

The younger generation is not the only one struggling. Thom Rainer, president and CEO of LifeWay Christian Resources, claims that the number one reason for declining church attendance is not that people are dropping out altogether, but that they are going less often.[4]

This is a symptom of a larger problem. There is a disconnect between what we have been taught about God and the life we are experiencing. We are led to believe that, if we receive Christ, all will be well and God will bless us. He will calm every storm, make us successful, and give us wonderful marriages and godly children. In essence, Christ will overcome every one of our problems, Christians will love us and receive us into their world, and we will be eternally happy. But when we begin to follow Christ, we find a different reality.

We still suffer hardships and we don't always see the blessing. We still have marital and family difficulties. We still fall into temptation. We suddenly find out that what we were taught to believe doesn't match what we are experiencing. As a result, we suffer from spiritual vertigo. Moreover, we become so accustomed to our condition that we adjust our lives to mediocre faith.

We are individually challenged to become a courageous hero who does great things for God; however, few of us believe we can be that person. We may want to do great things for God, but we do not see Him intervening in our everyday lives. We want to believe that He cares, but we just don't see the evidence. How can we step out with courageous faith if we feel He has let us down in the past?

How do we reconcile life and faith? How do we win over our doubts? How do we move forward with God when we feel like He will not come through for us? I wrote this book with a desire to help you work through these doubts and begin exercising courageous faith in your life.

Overcoming Spiritual Vertigo consists of four sections. The first defines faith and why it often conflicts with our life experiences. We will learn that what we see, hear and experience encompass *part* of the truth, but not the *whole* truth.

The second section addresses struggles in our personal faith. Here, we will discover how to overcome our primary challenges in that journey. The third section shows how to apply lessons from the first two and explains how to transfer our faith into lion-chasing, giant-killing courage. The final section will help you navigate your faith journey with clarity and boldness.

As you reflect on your life with God, I hope you will see how much He blesses you and realize that your faith is built to go the distance and accomplish great things in His name.

Part 1

The Challenge We Face

1

Regaining Our Spiritual Balance

*Future courage is based on our
ability to cope with present realities.*

C hris was a dedicated Christian and church leader. He willingly served the Lord by going on hospital visits, ministering to widows and supporting his pastor in moving the church forward. He spent many nights away from his family, visiting people who were sick or grieving the loss of a loved one. Chris also made great efforts to be the kind of husband and father that would be pleasing to God.

Fast forward one year—Chris is disillusioned with his faith and church life. During his most dedicated year of service, his wife had serious knee surgery, placing her on crutches for several weeks. He found himself being breadwinner, dad, nurse and part-time mom. Adding to that, his father had a stroke and suffered terrible mental difficulties. The year ended with Chris placing his father in a nursing facility because his violent outbursts became too much for home care. The man he called "Dad" was no longer the same man who had raised him.

His father had just passed away when Chris came to me for guidance. He was discouraged and admitted he doubted his faith. His reasoning was simple, one most of us can identify with. He said, "I felt I was doing the right things. I was a leader in the church and a good husband and father. I just can't believe a loving, heavenly Father would allow my dad to suffer as he did." I listened as Chris told his story. At the end of our conversation, he summed up his feelings by saying, "He may be a loving Father, but I feel like I treat my kids a lot better than He treats His." Chris was experiencing spiritual vertigo. His faith couldn't process what he was seeing, hearing or experiencing.

Contrast Chris' story with an inspiring book, *In a Pit with a Lion on a Snowy Day*. In it, author Mark Batterson uses Second Samuel 23:20, one of the most obscure Bible passages, to challenge his readers to exercise great courage:[1] "Then Benaiah the son of Jehoiada, the son of a valiant man of Kabzeel, who had done mighty deeds, killed the two sons of Ariel of Moab. He also went down and killed a lion in the middle of a pit on a snowy day."

Batterson sets the scene, describing Benaiah's confrontation with a five hundred-pound lion. Instead of running from it, Benaiah stares the lion down, causing it to run away. When the lion falls into a pit, Benaiah jumps down and kills it in terrifying hand-to-paw combat. It's a great read.

We often think courage is the metaphorical ability to chase lions and kill giants, but it also takes an enormous amount of courage to face the everyday challenges, hurts and disappointments in life. When we experience spiritual vertigo and become disillusioned with God, we are certain to face the future without faith.

We need courage to confront the unknown, move forward when faced with an opportunity, keep going when discouraged, and believe in the midst of suffering and loss. But where do we find this courage when our faith is struggling? Just as I needed water to help combat physical vertigo, we need spiritual fuel to overcome spiritual vertigo.

We find it in our relationship with Christ. I'm not saying that only believers possess courage. People often perform heroic acts without any faith in God. Our nation's history is filled with heroes from armed forces, law enforcement and first responders. They risk their lives every day to protect us. Even the entrepreneur possesses great courage, risking all to start a business or ministry.

This type of courage is based on our own resources—our abilities. What happens when we face insurmountable odds? What happens when life's challenges look like a five hundred-pound lion? What happens when we face illness, failure or loss of a loved one? What happens when we witness our parents losing their health or their minds? We are usually knocked off our spiritual balance. We simply will not boldly trust God with our future when we're unsure if He will come through for us.

Instead, we wonder, "Does God really care? Is He a loving, heavenly Father? Is He really there for me? If I truly give my life to Him, am I sure He will come through for me?" We think, "I cannot completely trust God because God might let me down."

When experiences challenge our faith, it is difficult to think about starting a new ministry, going out on the mission field, launching a new business or taking a public stand against injustice.

Our problem of spiritual vertigo is rooted not just in our beliefs about God, but in our beliefs in how God relates to us. How do you see God? What do you expect from Him?

Where Do We Begin?

The Starting Point: Our Salvation Experience

Our view of how God relates to us is first found in how we perceive our salvation experience. If we see our salvation as a miracle of God, we are on the right track. We may think, "Of course I believe my salvation is a miracle; I'm a sinner saved by grace." But what's your response when you hear that a prisoner who has committed heinous crimes has received Christ and changed his life? Do you doubt his experience? Do you think, "A man like that never changes? I wouldn't want him around my family." If so, it tells me that in some small way, you feel you deserve salvation. After all, you came from a good family, you grew up in church, and you haven't committed any horrible crimes or served prison time. You may not think you saved yourself, but being a good person doesn't hurt your chance of salvation either. In essence, you feel we use our own resources and good deeds to save ourselves.

On the other hand, you may think, "Praise God for the prisoner's salvation! I was a sinner myself and I don't know why God saved me. If anyone could look inside my mind, I would be seen as the worst of sinners. I have only God to thank and I feel overwhelmed by His grace."

Our attitude about our own salvation experience reveals much about how our faith operates. If we trust in our own resources and works for salvation, the greater the chances are that we believe the same way for our Christian walk. When we face a challenge that is beyond our resources, it throws us off our spiritual equilibrium. Then we wonder how we end up in our present circumstances and question why God doesn't intervene.

Our Expectations of God

How do you perceive your relationship with God? What are the roles? Who is the boss?

In their book *Cat and Dog Theology*, Bob Sjogren and Gerald Robison share an illustration that goes something like this: We all treat God the way cats and dogs treat us. When we get home from work or school, our dog greets us with great enthusiasm. Maybe he has a toy in his mouth, his tail is wagging and he is beside himself with excitement. Your cat, in contrast, does not greet you at all. He sits on the couch or runs from you, and dares you to touch him. It is almost as if you must earn the right to pet him or get his attention.

The theology is simple. A dog thinks, "Wow! This person loves me, feeds me and takes care of me—he must be God!" The cat thinks, "This person loves me, feeds me and takes care of me—I must be God!"[2]

Some of us live our lives to serve God; others live as though God is here to serve us. How we see our relationship with Him greatly affects our expectations of Him and that impacts our faith and our ability to trust Him.

Philip Crosby insightfully stated, "Quality is meeting expectations."[3] Where a person's opinions are concerned, I think that has some truth. For example, a new, cafeteria-style barbecue place in Orlando recently generated a lot of buzz. Many people urged me to try it out, claiming it was the best barbecue they'd ever tasted. So when my wife and I took their advice, we had high expectations of the food quality. We also weren't disappointed when we saw the line out of the door and had to pick up our food at the serving line, because we knew what to expect. The brisket was recommended and it was great; but we also ordered pork, which wasn't anything special. What would have happened if we'd expected a high-end restaurant with table service? Would our experience have been different if we had not ordered the brisket? The restaurant probably wouldn't have met our expectations and, consequently, we would have been disappointed in the quality.

We could use this same example at church. What if you see a church that appears to be formal and traditional but when you attend, you discover it's very contemporary? They might have the best music and teaching but if it's not what you expect, you may perceive it as low quality.

Unfortunately, the same can be true of our attitude about God. If we expect Him to be fatherly to us, if we expect life to go easy, if we feel we deserve God's blessings, if we think He is here to serve us, if we believe He has made promises He has not kept, then we will often be disappointed with God. We may reason, "If God is all-loving and all-powerful, shouldn't He treat me like I treat my children? Shouldn't He answer my prayers, bless me financially and keep me well?" This example of faith believes that if what we see, hear and experience is not what we expect from God, we cannot fully place our faith in Him. When our expectations are inaccurate and unrealistic, we will constantly battle spiritual vertigo.

You may have heard the saying, "You think the world revolves around you!" If you are like me, you're tired of that phrase. It's condescending and basically accuses someone of total self-centeredness. Most of us realize the world doesn't revolve around us, but we often subconsciously think God's world does.

Centuries ago, scientists believed that the earth was the center of the universe and all life revolved around it. Today we know the sun, not the earth, is at the center of our solar system. To operate properly, all the planets must revolve around the sun. If that stopped, all life would be in chaos. Planets and other heavenly bodies would collide into one another. Others would float off into oblivion. All life on earth would either freeze or be incinerated by heat. If life revolved around earth, the same would happen. The earth's gravitational pull is not sufficient to keep the solar system in order.

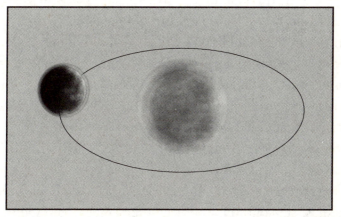

Fig. 1.

Let's imagine we are earth in this illustration[4] and Christ is the sun. As long as our lives are Christ centered, there is order and stability. Once life begins to revolve around us, disorder and chaos erupt.

Many modern churches and cultures lead us to believe that we are at the center. Churches often teach about positive self-esteem and your importance to God. (You *are* important to Him.) They teach that had you been the only sinner, Christ would still die for you. Since that is true, the assumption is that God's world must revolve around you—your needs, your prayers, your purpose in life.

Modern Western culture also teaches you to believe in yourself. Parents' lives often revolve around their children, making kids kings in many families. As a result, we often grow up as the center of attention. We reason (subconsciously) that since God loves us and is like our earthly parents, His world must revolve around us. As a result, we don't understand why He doesn't come through for us.

As important as we are to Him, God revolves around Himself. You are also not His only child. I am not His only child. As we pray, God is working in the lives of many other believers and nonbelievers, in different circumstances, for the best possible outcome that will bring Him glory. The Bible teaches us, "And we know that God causes all things to work together for good to those who love God, to those who are called according to His purpose" (Rom. 8:28).

We are here to bring Him glory. We are here to serve Him. We must step out in humility and remember that God is not on trial for His performance. He loves us and because of that, all the blessings we receive come from His grace. We are not natural children of God. We were adopted into His family because Christ died on the cross for us. "For you have not received a spirit of slavery leading to fear again, but you have received a spirit of adoption as sons by which we cry out, 'Abba! Father!'"(8:15).

If we believe God's world revolves around us, disappointment is inevitable. We will have expectations that God may not meet. Please realize some expectations are good when they are based on faith in what His Word teaches. When God makes a promise to us, it is an act of faith to expect Him to keep it. However, there are many expectations that are built on assumption and perceived promises that are not biblically based. We will discuss this in more detail in a later chapter.

What do we do? How do we apply our salvation experience to our everyday walk?

When we perceive God revolving around us, we become disappointed and often disillusioned with life. We reason that since God has not come through as we expected, trusting Him will cause failure, disappointment and embarrassment. We cannot be bold in our faith when we might fail.

What's My Next Step?

A few years ago, I went through a difficult time in life. Our church was in the process of building a new worship center and we were trying to raise $12 million in a capital stewardship campaign. We were also having some staff problems at the church. In the midst of all this, the worst thing of all happened—my wife was diagnosed with breast cancer.

I know the Bible teaches that God will never give you more than you can handle, but I felt I was past my limit. I always believed God gave me a high capacity for handling stress, but nothing of this magnitude had ever happened to me before. I was suffering through a bout of spiritual vertigo. I needed faith, courage and direction in my life.

It was through this need that I stumbled across a little book by C.J. Mahaney entitled *Living the Cross Centered Life*.[5] That book ministered to me much like I hope this book does for you. I found my salvation experience at the cross. It is also the place where I continue to find spiritual maturity and encouragement.

Jesus dying on the cross brought us freedom and forgiveness of sin.

Colossians 2:13–14 reads, "When you were dead in your transgressions and the uncircumcision of your flesh, He made you alive together with Him, having forgiven us all our transgressions, having canceled out the certificate of debt consisting of decrees against us, which was hostile to us; and He has taken it out of the way, having nailed it to the cross."

The apostle Paul wrote in Galatians 6:14, "But may it never be that I would boast, except in the cross of our Lord Jesus Christ, through which the world has been crucified to me, and I to the world."

Theologian John Stott said, "The cross is the blazing fire at which the flame of our love is kindled, but we have to get near enough for its sparks to fall on us."[6] C. J. Mahaney adds, "For me, grace is never more amazing than when I'm looking intensely at the cross, and I believe the same will be true for every child of God. There is nothing more overpowering and captivating to the soul than to climb Calvary's mountain with childlike attentiveness and wonder, with all the distractions and wrong assumptions cleared away."[7]

What then? After salvation, how do we find maturity and courage in the midst of trials? How do we live the Christian life? We find the answer in Colossians 2:6: "Therefore as you have received Christ Jesus the Lord, so walk in Him."

We received Christ by coming humbly before the cross. We offered no righteousness of our own. We simply threw ourselves at Jesus' feet and cried out for forgiveness and salvation. We came with no personal agenda or resume. We repented, turned from our sin and began to follow a new Master.

As the old hymn says, "Nothing in my hands I bring, simply to the cross I cling."[8]

We live the Christian life in the same way—at the foot of the cross. Each day that we humble ourselves before God, we cry out for His mercy. We honor Him as Lord. We revolve our lives around Him instead of hoping God will revolve around us. But how does the cross-centered life help us overcome spiritual vertigo?

First, living near the cross helps us experience a love relationship with Christ. Several years ago, I saw a painting of the crucifixion in the lobby of a church in Atlanta. The painting had three panels, each depicting one of the three who hung on the cross that day at Calvary: the thieves on each side and Christ in the middle. The picture was beautifully painted and large in its dimensions, but what was unusual about it was that there were no modesty towels. The depiction was graphic—the three men were totally naked. We were shocked to see it but one of my friends commented, "It makes you realize the shame and humiliation Jesus was willing to go through for us."

The Bible teaches that on the cross, He despised the shame and humiliation for us. He courageously did what He had to do.

When we sing about the cross, read about the cross, live beneath the cross, doubt diminishes and we see afresh how much God really loves us. He loved us enough to send His Son for us. As we become grateful for what He has done, we can better trust Him with our futures. In other words, my faith can process my circumstance if I know God loves me, if I feel His warmth and care for me.

Second, the cross declares our worth. Although God revolves around Himself, this doesn't diminish our value in Christ.

As the saying goes, two things ultimately declare the value of something: its owner and its worth. A few years ago, President John F. Kennedy's golf clubs sold for $772,500.[9] Recently, Elvis Presley's Bible went for $94,000 in the United Kingdom.[10] Those material items don't compare to the worth of a human life, especially in the eyes of God.

Before your birth, God counted you as valuable. "For You formed my inward parts. / You wove me in my mother's womb / I will give thanks to You, for I am fearfully and wonderfully made; / Wonderful are Your works, / And my soul knows it very well. . . . How precious also are Your thoughts to me, O God! / How vast is the sum of them!" (Ps. 139:13, 14, 17).

God loved you and had wonderful and precious thoughts of you long before you were born. However, value, as we learned above, is determined not only by who owned an item, but by how much someone is willing to pay for it. William Temple said, "My worth is what I am worth to God and that is a marvelous great deal, for Christ died for me."[11]

Even while we were enemies of God, Jesus died for our sins. That is how much we are worth to God; and God sets the standard for value. Why should we drown in our insecurities? How can we think God does not care? How could we think He wants us to fail? God declared us worthy! Though our present circumstances don't make sense to us, we know He has a future for us if He believes we are worthy. Romans 5:10 states it this way, "For if while we were enemies we were reconciled to God through the death of His Son, much more, having been reconciled, we shall be saved by His life."

Third, the cross clears our conscience. Jesus nailed our sin to the cross. "And He Himself bore our sins in His body on the cross, so that we might die to sin and live to righteousness; for by His wounds you were healed" (1 Pet. 2:24). We should not bear feelings of guilt, thinking God could not possibly bless us.

The visible circumstances of life may make it appear that the deck is stacked against trusting God; but as a believer, you can rest in the fact that God is on your side. Romans 8:32 says, "He who did not spare His own Son, but delivered Him over for us all, how will He not also with Him freely give us all things?" If God would give us Jesus to die on the cross, the rest is just a garnish to Him.

What if you gave your son to another family and, with tears and trembling when you hand your child over, they ask very humbly, "Can I have the stroller too?" As you look at them, you can tell they are worried about the stroller. They are overly concerned, fretting over the prospect of not getting the stroller. You might reply, "Well, of course, I am giving you my son—the stroller means nothing." We fret over strollers. If God gave us His Son, I think He would throw in all that came with the Son.

Since Christ saved you and forgave you of all your sins at salvation, He wants you to walk with Him and receive all the blessings He has for you. No matter what you have done, He desires to forgive and restore you.

Fourth, the cross helps us place ourselves in proper fellowship with God. Proverbs 28:1 says, "The wicked flee when no one is pursuing, / But the righteous are bold as a lion." Boldness refers to confident, courageous faith. When we are humbled at the cross, we realize that we are here to serve God, not here for God to serve us. We are already blessed beyond what we deserve. Our expectations of God become more biblically aligned and accurate. We become grateful for all He has given rather than focusing on what we feel is missing. It is at that point we can build a relationship with God as Lord of our lives.

Our greatest challenge is the mystery of how God relates to us; therefore, the closer we are to Christ, the more we will understand His relationship to us and how He works in our hearts.

It is probably easier for us to identify with Chris' spiritual vertigo than with the lion chasing Benaiah. Like Chris, we suffer from doubt, disillusionment and even despair. We cannot see ourselves as heroic figures for God because we often lack the courage to face disappointments in our lives.

As we step to the cross, we become aware of how much God loves us, how much He cares and how powerful He really is. God relates to us through love and grace, which are a privilege and blessing, and not one's right. By placing our faith in what Christ did on the cross, we begin to regain our spiritual balance.

Discussion Questions

1. What are your expectations of God and your relationship with Him? Are these expectations of Him found in the Bible? Do you feel He has broken a promise to you? Are you expecting something from God that you aren't sure has been promised?

2. In what area of your life do you have trouble trusting God (e.g., finances, healing, relationships, career, family)?

3. How will you humble yourself to be more like the dog who sees God as the One he serves and not the cat who expects God to serve him?

2

The Battle to Believe

When Linda walked into my office, I didn't know what to expect. She had previously written me a note questioning God and doubting her faith. The note, loaded with sarcasm, seemed somewhat cynical. I expected to meet a bitter, stern-faced woman ready to spew all her problems with God. To my surprise, Linda was a woman in her early forties with an upbeat and pleasant manner. However, as our conversation began, she emphatically shared that life had not been kind to her.

Her teenage son was physically challenged and her husband was an alcoholic. She had a friend in our church who was excited over an answered prayer that Linda considered trite. Her question was simple and fair: "Why does God care about answering prayers for church events or finding car keys but not have time to talk to me? I never remember having an answered prayer. Why should I trust Him anymore?"

Faith has a public relations problem. As that great theologian Archie Bunker once said, "Faith is believing what nobody would believe if it weren't in the Bible."[1] When tragedy occurs, a well-meaning friend may challenge you to "just believe" or "keep trusting God." You wonder if said friend has ever gone through any real problems.

Most of us can identify with the man who approached Jesus in Mark 9. "And Jesus said to him, 'If You can? All things are possible to him who believes.' Immediately the boy's father cried out and said, 'I do believe; help my unbelief'" (9:23–24). We vacillate between belief and unbelief every day.

At times, it seems that God's help is arbitrary. Why does He answer the prayer of one couple, blessing them with a long-awaited child, while another couple prays for years and never conceives? Why does one man get a promotion at work and another—who is just as faithful—get laid off? Why do we feel that we have prayed and struggled in faith, only to be disappointed by God? Why is one person healed of disease while another suffers?

Most of us have struggled with these questions. I have in my own experience. My most dramatic answer to prayer came to me as a college student. When I was eighteen, I was diagnosed with diabetes. The early discovery of the disease was a blessing because I could treat it by simply changing my diet. For four years, I was able to keep my sugar level under control by watching what I ate.

Then I began to cheat on my diet and by the time I was twenty-two, my doctor told me I had to start taking insulin shots. Not good news. Yet I had no one to blame but myself. I asked God to forgive my lack of discipline and accepted the consequences. Despite the diagnosis, I had a strange and wonderful peace about the situation.

Before I began taking the insulin, I had to go back to the doctor's office to take a three-hour test that would determine the level of insulin that I would need. The night before the appointment, I had a quiet, private prayer meeting with God. I was not praying about my physical condition at the time, but simply praying about various things God was laying upon my heart.

As I was talking to God, He revealed to me that He did not want me to have diabetes. In response, I prayed that God would supernaturally heal me of the disease. I did not go to a faith healer or make a special deal with Him. I simply asked.

I knew from the moment I said "amen" that God had healed me. The next day, I kept my doctor appointment. After they drew blood for the test, I went to hang out at the Baptist Student Union building on the university campus. It never occurred to me that God had not performed the miracle. I was at total peace.

After about three hours, I went back to the doctor's office. As I reached for the handle of the front door, the thought occurred to me, "What if I am not healed?" The momentary fear that startled my heart was not that I would have to take shots every day or perhaps die young. My fear was "if God has not healed me, what will it do to my faith?" I shook off the feeling of doubt and walked into the office. Immediately, my eyes met the nurse's as she was passing through the hall. She came toward me and before I had a chance to ask, she exclaimed, "You don't have it. I can't explain it, but your diabetes is gone!" Since that day more than thirty-five years ago, I am still free of the disease.

Soon after my healing, my doctor diagnosed me with Graves' Disease, a hyperactive thyroid condition. I don't mean to sound greedy, but I prayed hard for another healing. I think I prayed with more faith than I did over the diabetes. However, today my thyroid issues remain.

What is the answer? Why did He heal me one time and not the next? How do we know when to take a step of faith?

Our difficulty may be that we don't understand faith as God defines it.

What Is Faith?

In Scripture, we find a great and insightful book on faith entitled Hebrews, written to people immature in their faith and in danger of losing their passion for Christ. The writer warns his readers several times about drifting away from God.

"For this reason we must pay much closer attention to what we have heard, so that we do not drift away *from it*" (2:1).

"Do not harden your hearts as when they provoked Me,

As in the day of trial in the wilderness" (3:8).

"Concerning him we have much to say, and *it is* hard to explain, since you have become dull of hearing" (5:11).

Then, near the conclusion of the book, the writer issues a great challenge.

> But remember the former days, when, after being enlightened, you endured a great conflict of sufferings, partly by being made a public spectacle through reproaches and tribulations, and partly by becoming sharers with those who were so treated. For you showed sympathy to the prisoners and accepted joyfully the seizure of your property, knowing that you have for yourselves a better possession and a lasting one. Therefore, do not throw away your confidence, which has a great reward. For you have need of endurance, so that when you have done the will of God, you may receive what was promised.
>
> For yet in a very little while, he who is coming will come, and will not delay. But My righteous one shall

> live by faith; and if he shrinks back, My soul has no
> pleasure in him.
>
> But we are not of those who shrink back to destruction,
> but of those who have faith to the preserving of the soul.
>
> Now faith is the assurance of *things* hoped for, the
> conviction of things not seen. For by it the men of old
> gained approval.
>
> By faith we understand that the worlds were prepared
> by the word of God, so that what is seen was not made
> out of things which are visible. (Heb. 10:32-11:3)

Notice this passage reveals its subject matter early on in verse 35 with the word **confidence**. This word means "public courage." The premise is that it takes faithful perseverance demonstrated by public courage to receive the blessing of God. We read in Hebrews 10:36, "For you have need of endurance, so that when you have done the will of God, you may receive what was promised."

Looking further to chapter 11, verse 6, we see the key to pleasing God, "And without faith it is impossible to please *Him*, for he who comes to God must believe that He is and *that* He is a rewarder of those who seek Him."

How do we please God? In this verse, we find three components:

1. Come to Christ.
2. Believe that He is.
3. Believe that He will reward. He will ultimately come through for us regardless of the present situation.

Faith is the key to pleasing God and, ultimately, the courage to trust to the end, so we need to understand what God says about faith. Back up to Hebrews 11:1–3, and we find the only description of faith in Scripture, "Now faith is the **assurance** of *things* **hoped** for, the **conviction** of things **not seen**. For by it the men of old gained approval. By faith we understand that the worlds were prepared by the word of God, so that what is seen was not made out of things which are visible."

This passage begins with the concept of faith. In the Hebrew language, faith has the idea of future hope. The New Testament authors often refer to having hope. This can be confusing until we realize biblical hope is different from our definition of hope.

Our idea of hope has a measure of uncertainty: "I hope it will rain." "I hope I will get that promotion." In the Bible, hope is not merely wishful thinking but the idea of embracing a future we know will come and looking forward to receiving it. The faithful heroes of the Old Testament in Hebrews 11 had hope. It was a faith for the future.

This moves us into the first part of our description of faith. "Now faith is the assurance of things hoped for." Assurance is from the Greek word *hupostasis,*[2] meaning "substance or support." The idea is we have something solid undergirding us; in this case, someone we can count on. In Mark 11:24 Jesus said, "Therefore I say to you, all things for which you pray and ask, believe that you have received them, and they will be *granted* you."

Here, the word "believe" means it is as good as if the prayer has already been answered. Literally, "believe that you have already received it."[3] We find the same teaching in Hebrews 11:1. Then faith, first of all, means what we hope for in the future is as good as ours.

The second aspect of faith has to do with the unseen world. Faith is the conviction of things not seen. A "conviction" is a belief so deep that it alters our lives, leads our decisions and compels us to sacrifice. We are called to have a conviction of the things not visible to our eyes. Hebrews 11:2–3 clarifies this: "For by it the men of old gained approval. By faith we understand that the worlds were prepared by the word of God, so that what is seen was not made out of things which are visible."

There is a visible world seen with our physical eyes and there is an unseen, invisible world. The Bible speaks of the visible things being the temporary and the invisible being eternal. Second Corinthians 4:18 says, "Look not at the things which are seen, but at the things which are not seen; for the things which are seen are temporal, but the things which are not seen are eternal." Faith is the organ used for our spiritual sight. What we can see reveals some facts that are true in our lives. However, there are things we cannot see that are just as real and true.

In his book *God in the Dark*, Os Guinness says, "The known facts (what we see) are often against God, but that's not all the facts."[4] He goes on to say that what we see may be true, but it's only part of the truth. There is a truth that we cannot see. Only God knows the whole truth.

It may be true that you are jobless. It may be true that you are forty and lonely. It may be true that you are suffering from cancer. But it's not the whole truth. There is a future in an unseen world that only God knows. We can tap into this world of unseen truth by faith. Biblical faith is trust or confidence in God. We rely on God's knowledge and trust in His loving concern for us. We push forward knowing that He will deliver in the end. We discover what we see, hear or experience cannot always be trusted. Only God and His Word possess the whole truth.

Third, faith involves objective belief in a person's word. Hebrews 11:3 speaks of the world being formed by the word of

God. As we read Hebrews 11, we see Old Testament heroes trusting the word of God. Faith is not merely subjective because Scripture gives us objectivity and clarity.

Author and pastor Andy Stanley states, "Before we can act courageously, we must have clarity in a situation. If we are clear about the truth, we are then moved to action. We humans love ambiguity. We love to sit around and discuss ideas, solutions, and problems without reaching a conclusion. If we reach a conclusion, we feel we must act. If we have no clarity in a situation, then we feel justified over our inaction."[5]

This plays strongly into the philosophy of relativism, that all truth is relative. Whatever is true for you is your truth and whatever is true for me is my truth. This leads to the modern idea of tolerance. The old definition of tolerance meant that you could believe whatever you chose.

You had a right to be wrong; but because someone cared about you, they tried to help you see the truth. Today's definition of tolerance infers your truth is just as true as anyone else's, leading us to conclude that truth is arbitrary and subjective, that there is no absolute truth.

The result of this relativism is a lack of clarity leading to a lack of passion and a tendency toward inaction. Why act courageously? Why step out on faith? Why take chances if there is no gain? The purpose isn't worth the cost. We aren't compelled to act because we lack clarity of truth. The Bible gives us the truth, however. It says in Hebrews 1 that God has spoken; and since He cannot lie, I believe, receive and act on His Word.

A good, concise definition of faith is simply taking God at His Word. His promises to us are to be our only expectations of God. At times, it's hard to believe—it's hard to see by faith. When we lack understanding of faith, it cannot function properly.

Connecting the Dots: The Past

Faith is the connection of two worlds—the past and the future. It looks at God's past accomplishments and connects them to "biblical hope" for the future. God gave us the gift of faith, first received through His Word and then of course when we received Christ Himself into our lives. The Bible says in James 1:21, "In humility receive the word implanted, which is able to save your souls" and in First Peter 1:23, "For you have been born again not of seed which is perishable but imperishable, *that is*, through the living and enduring word of God." We have the organ of spiritual eyesight to look ahead with reliance, trust and confidence.

Imagine yourself as an illustration of faith. Stretch out your arms. Picture yourself reaching toward the past with your left arm and reaching toward the future with your right. Faith stands in the middle, connecting the two. Os Guinness would say, "Faith's calling is to live between times. Faith is in transit. It lives in an interim period. Behind faith is the great no longer. Ahead of it lies the great not yet."[6]

How does the "great no longer" help our faith? We look to the past with gratitude. Hebrews 10:32 tells us to remember the former days. Hebrews 11 helps us remember what the heroes of the past accomplished. The saints of the Old Testament often began a prayer with praise and thanksgiving. They weren't trying to flatter God but were building their faith for the task ahead through praise. The apostle Paul often began a letter with gratitude to God and to the people of the church.

"First, I thank my God through Jesus Christ for you all, because your faith is being proclaimed throughout the whole world" (Rom. 1:8).

"I thank my God always concerning you for the grace of God which was given you in Christ Jesus" (I Cor. 1:4).

"I thank my God in all my remembrance of you" (Phil. 1:3).

As we express gratefulness, we remember what God has done for us. This changes our attitude from entitlement to appreciation for what we have. Thanksgiving with humility combats the expectations we often place on God. It begins at the cross and should permeate our lives. Gratitude adjusts our faith to God's reality. It leads us to see the world from God's point of view.

I have heard it said we love 95 percent of things about our spouse but it's the 5 percent that drives us crazy. Why? Because we concentrate on what they lack rather than focus on what we love. When I was a young pastor, I received some great lessons on gratitude that I applied to a difficult funeral situation.

Just weeks after I started pastoring my first church, we held vacation Bible school. Like similar VBS programs, we enrolled many local children who didn't normally attend church. One of them was a five-year-old boy named Robin. A week after VBS, he and a friend were riding their tricycles on the sidewalk when a drunk driver veered off the road, hit Robin and killed him. Later, his parents told me how much Robin learned about Christ at VBS and how his heart was tender toward God.

A few days later, I had the task of preaching his funeral. I was twenty-six years old and this was only my third funeral. Talk about baptism by fire! What could I say from the pulpit that would bring comfort to his family? God brought to mind what I had learned a few years before about focus and thanksgiving. I began the message asking the congregation how long they felt a person should live—should it be sixty, seventy, eighty years? The Bible mentions three score and ten being an exemplary time. That's seventy years. In our minds, we felt Robin deserved to live out his seventy years. We concentrate on the sixty-five years we believe he lost and ask God, "Why?" Instead, I said, we needed to focus on the five years he had lived and the impact his love had on others. We should be grateful for the five years we had him. Our problem is the expectation of seventy years when God hasn't guaranteed any amount of time.

Later, I was able to lead Robin's parents, Grady and Phyllis, to faith in Christ. Robin was their only child and they had been told they could not have any more children. While all of that was true, it was not the *whole* truth. We prayed earnestly for the couple and God eventually blessed them with another son. The couple kept following Christ; and years later, Grady became ordained as a deacon in his church.

I mentioned previously that my wife, Pam, had been diagnosed with breast cancer. I remember vividly when and how I found out. We were on our way to her doctor for the result of the biopsy. She'd had scares before, so we were not overly worried. Earlier that morning, however, the doctor had called Pam to give her warning that the lump was indeed cancerous. On the road to his office, Pam broke the news to me. I was shocked. I couldn't believe it. I wish I could tell you that I responded in complete trust and confidence in God. I did not.

After a few comforting comments to Pam, I spent ten minutes in seething silence. I was mad at God. After all, Pam and I had been following Christ all our lives. We led many to Christ, we sacrificially served, we tithed and so forth (you know—the usual defense before God). We were in the worst, most stressful time at our church and now this.

As I turned into the parking lot of the doctor's office, God sent a sharp rebuke into my mind. It went something like, "You are not being grateful for what I have given. I gave you this great woman to be your wife for twenty-nine years. You do not deserve her. If I took her now, you would have had her for twenty-nine more years than you deserved." I focused on the future years I thought I might be cheated of instead of the twenty-nine years of blessing I already had. (God also added that I was being selfish.) Pam and I have been married for thirty-four years now and she is a breast cancer survivor. For this, I am grateful.

I'm not saying that we shouldn't suffer and grieve over loss, but gratitude goes miles in getting God off the hook for those maladies we blame on Him. Thanksgiving connects the dots to the future when we remember the great things God has done and we become excited about what He will do in the future. In Psalm 138, King David begins with thanksgiving.

"I will give You thanks with all my heart; / I will sing praises to You before the gods. / I will bow down toward Your holy temple / And give thanks to Your name for Your lovingkindness and Your truth; / For You have magnified Your word according to all Your name." Then in Psalm 138:3 he cites a result of his gratitude, "On the day I called, You answered me; / You made me bold with strength in my soul." It would seem his faith grew in verses seven and eight where he says, "Though I walk in the midst of trouble, You will revive me; / You will stretch forth Your hand against the wrath of my enemies, / And Your right hand will save me. / The LORD will accomplish what concerns me; / Your lovingkindness, O Lord, is everlasting; / Do not forsake the works of Your hands."

David reminded himself of God's past blessings and it caused him to realize that what God had done in the past, He could do in the future. What are you grateful for?

- If you woke up this morning with more health than illness, you are more blessed than the six million who will not survive this week.

- If you have never experienced the danger of battle, the loneliness of imprisonment, the agony of torture or the pangs of starvation, you are ahead of 500 million people in the world.

- If you can attend a church meeting without fear of harassment, arrest, torture or death, you are more blessed than three billion people in the world.

- If you have food in the refrigerator, clothes on your back, a roof overhead and a place to sleep, you are richer than 75 percent of people in this world.

- If you have money in the bank, in your wallet, and spare change in a dish someplace, you are among the top 8 percent of the world's wealthy.[7]

Why don't you stop reading and thank God for at least three things in your life?

1. _____

2. _____

3. _____

As we look to the past with gratitude, it changes our perspective on God and how He relates to us. It changes how we see God. Do you blame Him for your problems? Do you see God as guilty or innocent of abandonment in your life? If your grateful heart leads you to see His love, you will also be determined to see His hand at work in your present situation.

Suppose someone was on trial for murder and all the evidence pointed to their guilt. Every lawyer would see it as an open-and-shut case and the accused as guilty.

However, you believe in the man's innocence and would work diligently to find out all the facts. No matter where the evidence pointed, you would work hard to find the stone that was unturned, the missing witness, the DNA left at the crime scene.

Here we find an insight to faith. Evidence may point away from God's involvement in our circumstances, but that's not *all* the evidence. We know God is loving, full of grace and truth, and can always be trusted. So when I believe God is innocent of letting me down, I will look for evidence that proves Him trustworthy. I trust Him even when all evidence is against Him. I will believe Him for the whole truth.

In Psalm 62, King David's son Absalom had taken over David's kingdom. He was on the run, living in caves with a few of his followers. His anguish must have been great. His son rebelled against him. The people of Israel rejected him. It would have been easy to think that God no longer wanted him, the life he knew was over, and he faced a future of a gypsy. In Psalm 62:1–2 he cried out, "My soul *waits* in silence for God only; / From Him is my salvation. / He only is my rock and my salvation, / My stronghold; I shall not be greatly shaken." David knew that God is good. The evidence may have been against God, but David chose to wait for the whole truth. He proclaims in Psalm 62:7, "On God my salvation and my glory *rest*; / The rock of my strength, my refuge is in God."

Connecting the Dots: The Future

Again, gratitude helps put our lives in proper perspective. It replaces our sense of entitlement. If we don't deal with those feelings, we will eventually blame all of our problems on God.

So how do we reach forward with hope and confidence? The rest of this book explains the struggles we have in doing just that. Let me begin by sharing a basic, overruling concept:

The key to faith and all Christian life is to live under the active lordship of Christ.

First, let me remove confusion based on various opinions on when Christ became Lord.

We first receive Christ as Lord at our salvation experience. Romans 10:9–10 teaches "If you confess with your mouth Jesus *as* Lord, and believe in your heart that God raised Him from the dead, you will be saved; for with the heart a person believes, resulting in righteousness, and with the mouth he confesses, resulting in salvation." The word "Lord" means "master or ruler of my life." The moment we received Christ, we repented of our sins and surrendered our will to His.

We are supernaturally born again and become followers of Christ. There is no salvation without lordship or following God. When we receive Christ, we give all we know about ourselves to all we know about Christ. The problem is we don't know very much. As we grow in Christ, God gradually reveals different areas of our lives in which we need to surrender. We then make decisions on whether to surrender that area to Christ or no longer have Christ as active Lord of our lives. It's not that we lose our salvation if we say no, but we do lose His fellowship and peace.

Why is lordship crucial to our confidence in Christ? A sequence of events occurs in our lives, depending on who or what is ruling them.

1. We *choose* our master.
2. That master *controls* our lives.
3. We place our *confidence* in that master.[8]

One example of this is money. When we give money first place in our lives, it begins to control our decisions. Money becomes an idol to us. We then begin to think money can produce fulfillment, happiness and enjoyment in our lives—that money can deliver what we need and want. We believe it can be our rescuer. In essence, we place our confidence in it.

If we are going to place our confidence in God, we must place Him first in our lives. We must have Him as master of our hearts. The lordship of Christ is a foundational piece in "connecting the dots" of faith to the future. We are able to see that our relationship with Him is more important than any "thing" we want.

Our security is in Him. We can better see Him for who He is. The more we see, the more we can trust His character. We are not as tempted to blame Him for our troubles. We will not hold Him accountable for promises He has never made. We want His will done, not our own.

As we trust Him as Master, we begin to want what He wants for us. We begin to see the world through His eyes. When life does not go according to our expectations, we take comfort in knowing that the most important thing in our life—our relationship with Christ—can never be taken.

Therefore, we have nothing to dread or fear. We can boldly trust Him as we place Him first. David concludes our thoughts in Psalm 62:8 by encouraging us, "Trust in Him at all times, O people; / Pour out your heart before Him; / God is a refuge for us."

Is Christ Lord of your life? Who is your master? Some think if they follow Christ as Lord, then He replaces them on the throne of their lives. I think, however, we will discover that something else is already on the throne. It could be money, career, family, friends, even an addiction. But something else that we place first, that leads every decision, that gives us satisfaction, is already there.

That something is the voice deep within our soul that we allow to define who we are. If that voice is not God, then He must somehow fit into our plans, our priorities, and compete with our agendas. If He does not cooperate, we become disappointed with Him. That something else on our throne begins to control and enslave us. Jesus is the only person who will govern your life without enslaving you. He wants what's best for you and wants you to become all you can be.

What we see, hear or experience may not change; but in order to overcome spiritual vertigo, we must change our faith. It must realize its true character. We need to connect the dots between the *no longer* and the *not yet* in order to see life from God's perspective.

Discussion Questions

1. Review your thanksgiving list. Think about why you are grateful for these things and how God has blessed you.

2. Can you say that Christ is "active" Lord of your life? Are you ready to obey God no matter what you see, hear or experience?

3. Are you relying on anything besides a relationship with Christ to give your life meaning and satisfaction?

4. Why do you think you have trouble surrendering to God?

Part 2

The Struggles We Find

Chapter 3

Our Greatest Struggle

Often our greatest struggles in life are the struggles we have with God. I realize that our enemies are the world, the flesh, and the devil. However, we recognize those as adversarial to us. God, conversely, loves us and should be watching over us.

I have loved you with an everlasting love;
Therefore I have drawn you with lovingkindness.

Jeremiah 31:3

He who did not spare His own Son, but delivered Him
over for us all, how will He not also with
Him freely give us all things?

Romans 8:32

We ask ourselves, "If God loves me, why does He allow me to suffer through adversity?" We reason, "As my heavenly Father, shouldn't God be capable of controlling circumstances that prevent me from suffering and heartbreak? He holds the power, so why doesn't He love me enough to be in my corner or help me like a parent should?"

Rick Warren, author of *The Purpose Driven Life* and pastor of one of the largest churches in the world, recently lost his son to suicide.

How does a believer come to terms with that? Rick and his wife, Kay, served the Lord faithfully for years and continue to serve Him today. They influence people for Christ all over the world. Couldn't God protect their son?

One of my heroes in the faith was the late evangelist Ron Dunn. In his book *When Heaven Is Silent* he shared the story about his son Ronnie's suicide. He recalled how, in 1973, Ronnie's personality began changing.

With falling grades and drastic mood swings, Ron and his wife, Kaye, assumed Ronnie's problem was spiritual. They had no idea what was really happening. Finally, a doctor diagnosed him with bipolar disorder.

Ron and Kaye thought everything would be fine once the doctor placed Ronnie on medication. At last, they had answers—and an apparent solution. Ronnie could continue to pursue his ministry calling. Three months later, on Thanksgiving Day, Ronnie took his own life. Ron said, "When the casket was lowered into the earth, I buried with it a lifetime of easy answers and unasked questions—except one: *Why?*[1]

Something else made Ronnie's death more painful. Several family friends also had serious trouble with their teenagers; some were even arrested on drug charges. Bound by a mutual burden, the families formed a unique fraternity, prayed for each other, and believed God would honor their faith with answered prayers. Ron commented, "Ronnie was the only one who didn't make it. While God restored the others, it appeared He had ignored our prayers."[2]

In the last sentence, notice the deep struggle at the core of his faith. *While God restored the others, it appeared He had ignored our prayers.* What a heartbreaking statement. Who wouldn't be knocked off their spiritual balance? We know God holds the power and we know what we see is not the whole truth. Still, we struggle with the truth we do see and how God relates to us. Why is He silent at times? Why does He seem absent? Why does He put us through trials without showing us the way? Where is the God of the Bible? How can we reconcile our faith with the claims of Scripture?

Struggles with God are very common in Scripture. In Genesis 17:18, Abraham cried out, "Oh that Ishmael might live before You!" He battled with God, not the devil. Job battled with God—or how he perceived God was treating him. Satan was causing his problems. His friends were only making matters worse. However, his struggle was with God.

Kornelis Miskotte wrote about the horrors of Auschwitz in his book *When the Gods Are Silent.* He asks the chilling question: "One can still 'believe' in the God who permitted to happen what did happen, but can one still speak to Him?"[3] Does this seem cynical to you? Does it make you feel uncomfortable to question God?

There's nothing wrong with struggling; it's through our struggles that we understand God's ways. Your present circumstances may tell you that God is ignoring you and your prayers. Your adversity, in light of God's, might seem very true to you but it is not the whole truth. How do we resolve this conflict with God? Can we overcome spiritual vertigo?

In their book *In Search of a Confident Faith,* J. P. Moreland and Klaus Issler introduced a diagram on perspective.[4]

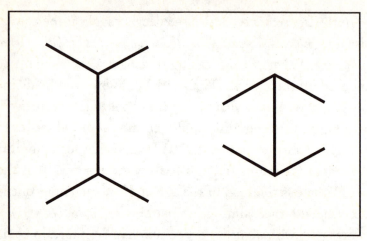

Fig. 2.

At first sight, the vertical lines appear to be different lengths. However, under closer examination, we find that they are actually the same. The direction of the horizontal lines changes our perspective, just as our horizontal circumstances change our vertical perspective with God.

Two people witnessed adversity. One man, called to ministry, saw his sister suffer before she died of cancer. He lost his faith. Now a declared atheist, he becomes a multimillionaire and gives his fortune away to non-Christian, and often anti-Christian, causes. Another person went on a mission to Central America, where he witnessed poverty, disease, paganism and social horrors. He returned home with a grateful heart for all God's blessings and vowed to spend his life as a missionary making a difference. Two men, two experiences, two perspectives, two very different outcomes.

In this chapter, I want to challenge your perspective on life. To overcome our struggles with God, we must see faith and life from God's perspective. When we see life vertically, rather than horizontally, we ask ourselves, "Through my struggles, what is God trying to do in my life?"

The Man Who Wrestled with God

The message in Genesis 32 helped me through many times of struggle. Jacob was the second-born of twins. He grabbed his brother's heel as he came of out of the womb, so his parents named him Jacob, meaning "heel-grabber." But the name also means "swindler." He and his brother, Esau, were the sons of Isaac and the grandsons of Abraham. Esau was a man's man. He was the kind of guy who hunted, fished, worked out and played football. The Bible also says he was very hairy. Jacob, on the other hand, was the kind of guy who helped his mom around the house, more of a *Better Homes and Gardens* kind of guy.

After a day of hunting, Esau came home famished. Jacob was cooking lentil stew and Esau insisted that Jacob give him some. Jacob agreed on the condition that Esau sell his birthright, and all the rights and authority that went with it, in exchange. Esau agreed. (That must have been some good stew!) The Bible teaches that Jacob stole Esau's birthright.

A few years later, their father, Isaac, believed that he was dying and wanted to pronounce a final blessing on Esau, his eldest (and favorite) son, as tradition dictated. Isaac's wife, Rebekah, schemed with Jacob (her favorite) to steal the blessing. While Esau was out hunting venison for Isaac, Rebekah dressed Jacob to look and feel like Esau. The disguise fooled Isaac, who was nearly blind, and he gave the blessing to Jacob. When Esau discovered the deception, he was so infuriated that he vowed to get even with his brother. Rebekah, fearing for Jacob's life, convinced him to flee to the household of her brother, Laban.

Jacob lived in Laban's household for twenty years. Laban had two daughters—the eldest, Leah, and the younger, Rachel. Jacob fell in love with Rachel from the moment he met her. He made a deal with Laban to work for seven years in exchange for Rachel's hand in marriage. At the end of seven years, Laban swindled Jacob and gave him Leah in marriage.

When Jacob discovered this deception, he pleaded with Laban to make good on his original deal. Laban agreed, on the condition that Jacob work seven more years in exchange for Rachel. I guess Jacob reaped what he had sown.

After twenty years in Haran, Jacob wanted to return home to his family. Genesis 32 finds Jacob fearful of his impending confrontation with Esau. He was so scared that he sent his servants and livestock ahead, hoping to soften Esau's heart.

Verses 22–23 say, "He arose that same night and took his two wives and his two maids and his eleven children, and crossed the ford of the Jabbok. He took them and sent them across the stream.

And he sent across whatever he had." Jacob sent gifts ahead and placed his family in front of him, hoping Esau would not take his revenge.

Genesis 32 recounts the familiar story of Jacob wrestling with God. It is an Old Testament illustration of a person's struggle with the Lord. Genesis 32:24–25 states, "Then Jacob was left alone, and a man wrestled with him until daybreak. When he saw that he had not prevailed against him, he touched the socket of his thigh; so the socket of Jacob's thigh was dislocated while he wrestled with him."

As we spiritually wrestle with God, we learn spiritual lessons. In the midst of our struggles, we must recognize what

God is doing in our lives. What are God's purposes when we go through our battles with Him?

What Is God Trying to Do?

When I experience spiritual vertigo, it helps me to know that God is always working in my life. When I am off my spiritual balance, He remains balanced; but what is He trying to accomplish in my life? There may be one of four reasons God may be bringing trials in your life:

- Brokenness
- God desires to change our lives
- To take us through darkness to a place of blessing
- Spiritual Maturity

Brokenness

The first concept in our discussion is brokenness. Roy Hession first introduced this concept to me in his book *The Calvary Road*.[5] Brokenness takes us to a place of humility before God and the Calvary road is the path to the cross-centered life.

I remember watching old westerns when I was a little boy. I especially liked watching the breaking of the horses. These stories usually showed a cowboy who caught the fastest, most beautiful and most spectacular horse on the prairie. However, the horse was useless until tamed or saddle broke. The cowboy mounted the horse only to be bucked off time after time. I'd cheer for the hero as he continually got back on the horse. He never gave up until the horse was broken. Only then could he use the horse as intended. We are like those special horses. We have enormous potential; but until we are broken, we can't fulfill God's purpose for our lives.

Dr. Charles Stanley, pastor of First Baptist Church Atlanta, presents another brokenness analogy. In John 12, Jesus visited the home of Lazarus, Mary and Martha in Bethany. Mark tells the moving story of Mary anointing Jesus while he visited their home. She broke a vase that released perfume onto Christ's head. The perfume inside the vase was worth eleven months' wages. The vase, however, had little value and was nearly worthless considering its contents. Dr. Stanley compared the vase to our flesh. The perfume is the life of Christ who lives within every Christian. In order to get to the best stuff, the outer shells must be shattered.[6]

A friend once advised me that, before I call a new minister on staff, I should make sure he has gone through brokenness. If he hasn't, I should be prepared to go through brokenness with him. A. W. Tozer said, "It is doubtful whether God can bless a man greatly until He has hurt him deeply."[7]

Some believe the man who wrestled with Jacob was an angel, others believe he was an Old Testament appearance of Christ. Either way illustrates a man wrestling with God. Near daybreak, the heavenly being pulled Jacob's hip bone out of the socket. Jacob would forever walk with a limp, reminding him of the night he wrestled with God.

From that moment forward, he could no longer rely on his own strength. He couldn't fight his own battles. He became humbly dependent on the Lord. Jacob had to be broken before God.

Why does God put us through brokenness? Why doesn't He rescue us from all adversity and bless us? We can't save ourselves from sin. God saved us at the cross; therefore, we must depend on Christ to live a Christian life that glorifies Him. When we came to Christ at salvation, God saved us through

His grace. Ephesians 2:8–9 says, "For by grace you have been saved through faith; and that not of yourselves, *it is* the gift of God; not as a result of works, so that no one may boast." If we are to live a Christian life, magnifying Christ and fulfilling our purpose, we must do it by His power and grace.

How do we receive this grace? As in our previous study about the cross, it comes down to humility. We find an example of this in the life of the apostle Peter. Before he first met Jesus, he was a fisherman. When he began to follow Christ, he changed but still remained very self-centered. He was usually the first to speak up in a crowd; he was the one who walked on water, and was the leader of the original apostles.

Peter declared he would never deny Christ. But after Jesus' arrest, he did just that—three times. Devastated, Peter lost his self-confidence. Upon His resurrection, Jesus told the women at His tomb to go and tell the disciples to meet Him. He singled Peter out, saying, "Be sure you retrieve Peter for Me." After this, Peter was a changed man.

Peter would no longer be led by his pride and self-confidence. He was prepared to receive the indwelling of the Holy Spirit and greatly impact the world for Christ. This, of course, took place later in the second chapter of Acts on the day of Pentecost.

What are you going through today? What adversity is striking you down? Do you feel small because you can't find work? Do you feel like you failed as a mother because of the lives your grown children are leading? Did someone say something that hurt your feelings? Are you frustrated because of circumstances out of your control?

It's possible that God is sending you through a period of brokenness. We all experience those times because of our tendency to veer away from the cross. Our brokenness calls us back to a humbled, cross-centered life. It breaks the outer shell—the vase—to retrieve the sweet perfume aroma on the inside.

God Desires to Change Us

Romans 8:29 teaches, "For those whom He foreknew, He also predestined to *become* conformed to the image of His Son, so that He would be the firstborn among many brethren."

God predestined (or preplanned) every believer's transformation to the image of His Son. The two primary ways God changes us are through internal and external pressure.

Internal pressure comes from the Holy Spirit, who uses God's Word and prayer to bring about change in our lives. When we listen to Him, He reveals where we need to change through the convicting power of His Word.

If only life were that simple. Sometimes we don't listen to the inner prompting of the Spirit. Sometimes we harden our hearts to God's Word. God uses a second avenue for change. He chooses to bring change through external pressure. He brings trials, adversity and disappointments that minister to us. He wants to change us. Adversity is often the only way to bring about that change.

Our problem from the outset is that we hate change. A pastor was talking to a hundred-year-old man. He commented that the old man had seen more change in his lifetime than any other generation in history. The man replied, "Yep, and I was agin' (against) every one of them."

I think the only people who like change are wet babies, and even they are often pretty reluctant. We are not only against change in our world and culture, but in our personal lives as well. We have heard the saying "no one is perfect" but when someone tries to tell us we aren't, we are offended. We know we haven't reached perfection. We need to grow. In order to grow, we must change.

The story of Jacob continues in Genesis 32:26–28, "Then he said, 'Let me go, for the dawn is breaking.' But he said, 'I will not let you go unless you bless me.' So he said to him, 'What is your name?' And he said, 'Jacob.' He said, 'Your name shall no longer be Jacob, but Israel; for you have striven with God and with men and have prevailed.'"

I mentioned previously that Jacob's name means "swindler" or "heel-grabber." The actual Hebrew word here means "deceiver."[8] This same Hebrew word is found in Jeremiah 17:9 where it says, "The heart is more deceitful than all else / And is desperately sick; / Who can understand it?" When Jacob gave his name, he actually said my name is "deceiver." The Lord replied, "Your name is no longer 'deceiver' but 'Prince of God' (Israel)." However, as we soon learn, God not only changed his name, but also his character.

God changed Jacob's name and character after one intense night of wrestling. For us to change, pressure must often come to bear. What causes us to change?

We change when hurt forces us to change.

Like Jacob, who experienced great pain as his hip went out of joint, we must often experience hurt or disappointment before we're willing to change. Sometimes, we endure pain greater than the pain of change. Dr. Howard Hendricks relates this in his book, *The Battle of the Gods*.

It is amazing how difficult it is for the Lord to break through to us in certain areas. I used to pray for years as a father, *Lord, change my children.* And nothing happened. I used to go into my study at the seminary and throw myself across the desk and say, *O Lord, overhaul my students.* And nothing happened.

Then I began to see that my prayer must be changed, *Lord, change my children's father. Change my students' professor.* And when God was pleased to do that, I saw remarkable, dramatic changes in my children and in my students.[9]

We change when we see enough to realize that we have to change.

When Jacob admitted his name was "deceiver," he saw himself as he really was: "I have lived my life by deception, trickery and deceit. That is who I am." We also see an example of this in the life of Peter. The Bible says when Jesus saw Peter and other disciples fishing, they hadn't caught anything all day. He told them to cast their nets on the other side of the boat (see John 21:1-6). If Peter could give us his testimony of this event, it might read something like this:

> *It was a frustrating and uneventful day. We caught nothing. We had mouths to feed and bills to pay. Maybe tomorrow, we said. But then I saw Jesus coming toward us. My disposition immediately changed. I didn't want Him to see me so irritated and angry. He asked me how the day had gone and when I replied, He told me to cast my nets on the other side of the boat. I thought,* I'm the fisherman here. Doesn't he think we already tried that? We are at shore; there's no fish here. But I guess I'll humor Him. *So we cast the nets on the other side of the boat. The catch was so large we*

couldn't pull it out of the water. Our nets began to break. I had to call men from other boats to help us. Then I turned to Jesus with a big, dumb grin on my face. But when I looked into His eyes, I really saw Him for the first time. I saw Him for who He was. I also saw myself for who I was. With a brokenness of soul and with all I had, I dropped to my knees and begged Him to depart from me because I knew I was a sinful man. I had no right to be in His presence.

When we gaze upon our Savior and see Him for who He is, it is then we will see ourselves for who we really are. We will be motivated to change.

We change when we are close enough to want change.

"So he said to him, 'What is your name?' And he said, 'Jacob.' He said, 'Your name shall no longer be Jacob, but Israel; for you have striven with God and with men and have prevailed'" (Gen. 32:27–28).

Jacob wanted to know the name of the heavenly being he was wrestling. He was close physically, but he was also close spiritually and wanted to know more. When we get close to God, close to the truth, desires will change.

I heard about a high school principal having trouble with a few teenage girls. Every day, a few of them would go into the restroom, put on heavy lipstick and kiss the mirror, leaving their lip prints for custodial workers to clean. After discovering who the girls were, the principal marched them into the restroom. He asked, "You see all this lipstick?" They each grinned and nodded. He said, "Watch this. This is what our janitor must do every day to clean this off." He turned to the janitor, who dipped his mop in the toilet and began to wash off the mirror. He never found lipstick on the mirror again. The young ladies saw the truth and they were motivated to change their behavior.

In college, God began to do a work in my life. I started hanging out with a few people from a campus ministry. They would read the Bible and then, in general conversation, discuss what they read. At the time, I was not reading the Bible. But I didn't want anyone asking what I'd read and not have an answer, so I started reading it. Within a few weeks, I found that reading the Bible became a great desire in my life. Not only did I find the Bible fascinating, but I also felt God was speaking to me in a very personal way. I grew closer to God. A change took place in my life that was so profound that I never looked back. I am who I am today in large part due to that change in my life.

We change when we pray enough for it.

In Genesis 32:26 we read, "Then he said, 'Let me go, for the dawn is breaking.' But he said, 'I will not let you go unless you bless me.'" I would describe this cry as a comparison to wrestling with God in prayer. When we desire something so much from God, we call out to Him. Jacob wrestled with God all night. Until this point in his life, Jacob received his blessings illegitimately. He deceived his father and stole Esau's blessing. All his life, I think, he just wanted God's approval and probably his dad's as well. He then trusted God to give him what he needed. It is the only time in Scripture that an individual works for God's blessing. It reminded me of when Jesus said in Matthew 7:7–8, "Ask, and it will be given to you; seek, and you will find; knock, and it will be opened to you. For everyone who asks receives, and he who seeks finds, and to him who knocks it will be opened."

We change through God's grace.

Ultimately, only God changes us. Jacob was changed when God changed him, not when Jacob changed himself. Only by God's grace do we come to terms with sinful habits, negative attitudes, or fears that keep us from moving forward with Him. This grace, again, only comes through a humble heart.

Where do you need change? Where are you struggling? Are you wrestling with anger, depression, indulgence, lack of passion, lack of hunger for God's Word, fear in sharing the gospel? Whatever you are struggling with, God wants to change you so that He can do a greater work in your life. Struggling with God is often the avenue to this greater work. Still, there is another possible reason why God leads us to change.

To Take Us Through Darkness to the Place of Blessing

Suffering tends to isolate us. If we go through a cancer diagnosis, we yearn to speak with someone who has already experienced it. Why? Because our suffering makes us feel alone. If a loved one dies, friends and family surround us, yet we still feel isolated.

Jacob once swindled and deceived others. After wrestling with God, he became God's champion. He would go on to father twelve sons, and from those sons would come the twelve tribes of Israel. God used that nation to inspire and teach us from their history, preserve the Bible through the centuries, and bring Christ into the world.

We find a new, courageous Jacob, one who would later meet his brother with faith and humility. Before, he sent his family and herdsmen out before him (to a possible death). After, he boldly stood before Esau himself.

Second, like Jacob, we should be encouraged that through our struggles we can receive the greatest blessing of all. Several years ago, my oldest son, Brandon, left for Liberty University to play golf and study business—in that order. Brandon was an athlete in high school. His game was basketball. He played point guard on a team that won 102 of 106 games over a two-year period. At the end of his freshman year, he broke his leg at the growth plate. After much rehabilitation, he returned the following season. He rebounded from an injury from which few athletes recover.

The next season started well, but then the bottom fell out. I did all I could not to miss a game, but occasionally it was unavoidable. I was at our annual men's retreat one such time. In between sessions, I anxiously called my wife for a report on the game. When I asked her how he did, she said, "He did okay." That didn't sound good. As we continued to talk, it sounded like he struggled throughout the game. "An off night," I concluded.

I managed to attend the next game and I was very surprised. Brandon struggled to dribble the ball up the court and his shots and passes were off. I asked him after the game, "What happened?" He said, "Dad, I can't straighten my arms." The next day, my wife took him to the doctor. He was diagnosed with juvenile rheumatoid arthritis. Although he was able to finish the season, his basketball career was over.

Fortunately, he also enjoyed golf. When we first moved to Florida, some members of our church decided to put together a men's golf tournament. I had the privilege of starting the tournament with the first shot. I guess they figured since I could play a little basketball and softball that golf shouldn't be a problem. (I hadn't played in so long I had to borrow clubs.) I walked to the first tee with more than a hundred players gathered on each side of the tee box. I took a deep breath, swung big, shanked the shot, and almost took the head off one of our church members.

Soon after that, one of our church members gave me a new set of clubs and three hundred new golf balls. Another member, wanting to help, gave me a summer membership to the local country club. (I guess they were even more embarrassed than I was about my game.) My two sons and I lost every one of those three hundred golf balls on that course.

Fast forward a few years and Brandon became a collegiate golfer. Instead of playing in the NBA, he dreamed of joining the PGA Tour. After a season of golf, however, he realized that his dream of being a professional golfer wasn't likely to come to fruition. Golf became so time-consuming that he eventually had to choose between the game and school. He chose school—a wise decision. During that time, his relationship with his high school girlfriend ended. The future he planned collapsed and he wondered, "What now?"

Brandon went into a time of deep reflection. He read the Bible so much that his friends wondered if he was becoming too "spiritual." It was during this time that God called him into the ministry. I say all of this to tell you what he shared with me as he ended his struggle with God. He said, "Dad, we talk about the blessings of God, but could the greatest blessing of all be the presence of God Himself?"

Psalm 16:11 says, "You will make known to me the path of life; / In Your presence is fullness of joy; / In Your right hand there are pleasures forever." Brandon discovered that the presence of God trumps anything we see, hear or experience. He became closer to God than ever. It was the turning point in his life. God became his greatest gift. Sometimes we think God is just throwing trash our way. Often our problem is discerning the treasure from the trash.

A man browsing through a bookstore noticed some old books that he thought looked overpriced. He told the clerk, "Wow, my grandmother just died and I was rummaging through her attic, I found a large collection of old books that I threw away. One was an old Bible."

The clerk responded, "You should have saved it. I'm sure it was worth some money."

The man replied, "Yes, it was a Guten-something-Bible."

The clerk gasped. "A Gutenberg Bible?"

"Yes, a Gutenberg Bible," the man nodded.

"That thing is worth over ten thousand dollars," the clerk replied.

"Not this Bible," said the man. "Some guy by the name of Martin Luther wrote all over it."

Just like that man, many of us don't recognize God's treasures in the midst of what we think is trash.

Spiritual Maturity

God's end goal is to bring us to spiritual maturity and He may use trials and adversity to do it. James 1:2–4 (NIV) tells us, "Consider it pure joy, my brothers and sisters, whenever you face trials of many kinds, because you know that the testing of your faith produces perseverance. Let perseverance finish its work so that you may be mature and complete, not lacking anything."

This is true not only from a spiritual point of view, but from an emotional maturity standpoint as well. When we rescue our children from every trial or buy them toys (and larger items later) to make life easier or to combat disappointment, we raise an emotionally challenged adult. My generation treated their kids like kings. Our world revolved around attending their various activities, buying them designer shoes and clothes, taking them on special trips, defending their actions with teachers and coaches, and generally doing all we could to save them from unhappiness. As a result, many of the children in my generation have grown up to find that the world is not as compliant as their parents. They often continue believing the world still revolves around them, and, as a result, they become disillusioned and disappointed with life.

What we as parents want most for our children's happiness can become elusive for them. Some parents often shower their children with good things and allow them to have their way because not only do they *want* their children's love, they seem to *need* it.

God is a wiser parent. He loves us, but He does not need our love in return. No matter how much we cry, beg or manipulate, He will only give us what is best for us. He allows the trials and troubles in our lives to mature us emotionally and spiritually. It's encouraging to know that in the midst of my doubt (spiritual vertigo), God is at work in my life. He is at work in yours too.

Discussion Questions

1. Do you feel like you have a problem that God is not big enough to remove?

2. Think about a problem in the past. How did you respond? What did God do in your life as you confronted that problem?
3. Think about the challenges you are facing. List the actions you think God might be taking in your life.

4

The Performance Trap

Sometimes those who go through the tragedy of divorce are reluctant to try marriage again. Kathy had known her marriage was in trouble for years. In spite of her prayers, her husband eventually left her for another woman. She was heartbroken. After years of hurt and grief, she wanted a new beginning. However, past performances left her with trust issues.

How could she trust another man? She trusted someone with her whole heart and look how it ended. Could she trust her own judgment in another relationship? She felt like a failure. She felt unwanted but she also felt like she could have been a better wife.

In some ways, she felt she drove her husband away. She felt unlovable and thought maybe she wasn't wife material. How could she trust God again? She prayed so hard before. She believed she had trusted God with her marriage. She knew God was there, just maybe not for her.

Many of us have faced similar doubts in our lives. When we were young, trusting others came naturally. After life unfolds, it is not so easy. Our past determines our ability to trust Him. In order to overcome our spiritual vertigo, we must deal with ourselves, others and God.

Disappointments in life are real. Our early days in school tend to begin with confidence. However, in a few short weeks, we often become content with simply being invisible. Our disappointments and embarrassments affect us in very negative ways. Most believers similarly begin their walk with faith and courage, only to later walk with caution and timidity because of perceived failures or disappointments.

I can't tell you how many times I've heard older Christians laugh at the zeal of a new believer. "Just wait. He'll mellow out," they'll say. But do they really mean, "Just wait. He'll become just as mundane and domesticated as I am"? Our loss of passion and trust is often the result of being disappointed with life and disillusioned with God's performance, the performance of others and our own personal failures. In other words, we think, "It's hard to trust when we know better."

When we think about performance, we are comparing the effort and outcome to the perceived expectations we have placed on certain individuals. We seem to place ourselves in a position to judge God, others and ourselves. I am not saying this is right. It's just what we do. This is reality for most, and a negative performance review hurts our faith.

When gnawing feelings about the past nibble at the heart of our faith, we wonder if we deserve God's blessings. We reason, "I know God is all-powerful; therefore, it must be me, my lifestyle and my shortcomings." Other people's performances may cause us to doubt whether God can or will intervene in their lives.

We ask ourselves, "Can I be content if my loved ones are outside God's will? Will God bypass their free will? What will He do? What can He do? God's past performances may also give us cause to wonder if He will rescue us. Will we get the job? Conceive? Be healed? Seize the opportunity? After all, lions have sharp teeth. Who wants to jump into a pit and be mauled? Yet God wants us to see life through His eyes. He wants to encourage us. He does not want us to walk in spiritual vertigo. He wants to do something great in our lives.

Returning to the book of Hebrews, we find a great source of hope through the life of Moses.

> By faith Moses, when he had grown up, refused to be called the son of Pharaoh's daughter, choosing rather to endure ill-treatment with the people of God than to enjoy the passing pleasures of sin, considering the reproach of Christ greater riches than the treasures of Egypt; for he was looking to the reward. By faith he left Egypt, not fearing the wrath of the king; for he endured, as seeing Him who is unseen. By faith he kept the Passover and the sprinkling of the blood, so that he who destroyed the firstborn would not touch them. By faith they passed through the Red Sea as though *they were passing* through dry land; and the Egyptians, when they attempted it, were drowned. (11:24-29)

This Hebrew passage is a commentary on Moses' life, which began in Exodus 2. Moses was born to a woman named Jochebed. During this period in history, Pharaoh grew fearful of the Jewish slaves. They multiplied rapidly and he feared their potential power. Therefore, he ordered the death of all Jewish male children at birth. Exodus 1:17–19 reads:

> But the midwives feared God, and did not do as the king of Egypt had commanded them, but let the boys live. So the king of Egypt called for the midwives and said to them, "Why have you done this thing, and let the boys live?" The midwives said to Pharaoh, "Because

the Hebrew women are not as the Egyptian women;
for they are vigorous and give birth before the midwife
can get to them."

Pharaoh ordered the midwives to kill the male children. But some, including Jochebed's midwife, refused the order, thus saving Moses' life. Jochebed placed baby Moses in a basket on the Nile at the same time she knew Pharaoh's daughter would be coming to the river. Pharaoh's daughter found baby Moses and raised him as her own.

As Moses grew up, he began to identify with the Israelites. One day, he saw an Egyptian beating an Israelite, so he killed the Egyptian. He thought he would be a hero. Instead, his people turned against him as he ran for his life. We see the New Testament commentary of Moses' decision in Hebrews 11:25: "choosing rather to endure ill-treatment with the people of God than to enjoy the passing pleasures of sin."

The Faith Acts of Moses

Look at all of Moses' acts of faith:

- By faith he refused his Egyptian upbringing (Heb. 11:24).
- By faith he endured persecution with his own people rather than live in the luxury of the Egyptian palace (Heb. 11:25).
- By faith he looked to a greater reward than worldly riches (11:26).
- By faith he saw Him who was unseen (11:27).
- By faith he kept the Passover so that the firstborn of Israel would not die (11:28).
- By faith he passed through the Red Sea on dry land (11:29).

It's easy to look back and think, "Well, Moses spoke directly to God at a burning bush. Moses saw great miracles. Moses was a great man. God loves Moses more than He loves me.

However, keep in mind that Moses felt the pressure and doubt of his past performances too. He killed a man in an act of heroism and he ended up spending forty years in what Exodus 3:1 of the King James Bible calls "the backside of the desert." Not sure where that is, but it sounds bad. I'm sure he didn't feel very blessed.

Yet God blessed Moses and He wants to bless you. I define a blessed life as "a life that experiences the presence of God." How would you define it? Would your description mean everything works out well for you? Romans 8:28 promises "God causes all things to work together for good to those who love God, to those who are called according to *His* purpose."

Would you define yours as an emotionally whole and generally happy life? Galatians 5:22–23 tells us that *is* the Christian life: "But the fruit of the Spirit is love, joy, peace, patience, kindness, goodness, faithfulness, gentleness, self-control; against such things there is no law."

God gives you this and so much more. Romans 8:32 has this promise: "He who did not spare His own Son, but delivered Him over for us all, how will He not also with Him freely give us all things?"

We hear the phrase "in all things God wants to bless us," but we can't always see that. We see what we perceive as the truth. We may realize it's not the whole truth, but is the rest any better? Will God rescue us? Do we deserve to be rescued? Let's look at the barriers of past performances.

Our Past Performance

We read the background of our story in Exodus 3:1–10.

> Now Moses was pasturing the flock of Jethro his father-in-law, the priest of Midian; and he led the flock to the west side of the wilderness and came to Horeb, the mountain of God. The angel of the LORD appeared to him in a blazing fire from the midst of a bush; and he looked, and behold, the bush was burning with fire, yet the bush was not consumed. So Moses said, "I must turn aside now and see this marvelous sight, why the bush is not burned up." When the LORD saw that he turned aside to look, God called to him from the midst of the bush and said, "Moses, Moses!" And he said, "Here I am." Then He said, "Do not come near here; remove your sandals from your feet, for the place on which you are standing is holy ground." He said also, "I am the God of your father, the God of Abraham, the God of Isaac, and the God of Jacob." Then Moses hid his face, for he was afraid to look at God.
>
> The LORD said, "I have surely seen the affliction of My people who are in Egypt, and have given heed to their cry because of their taskmasters, for I am aware of their sufferings. So I have come down to deliver them from the power of the Egyptians, and to bring them up from that land to a good and spacious land, to a land flowing with milk and honey, to the place of the Canaanite and the Hittite and the Amorite and the Perizzite and the Hivite and the Jebusite. Now, behold, the cry of the sons of Israel has come to Me; furthermore, I have seen the oppression with which the Egyptians are oppressing them.

> Therefore, come now, and I will send you to Pharaoh,
> so that you may bring My people, the sons of Israel,
> out of Egypt.

Moses had been shepherding his father-in-law's flocks for many years. As he led them, he came to Mount Horeb, the mountain of God. It was there God appeared in the burning bush and announced that He would make Moses a great leader and a courageous hero.

If we took the "unbroken" Moses from forty years prior, he would have felt up to the task. Maybe he would have thought, "It's about time. I was wondering when God would give me an opportunity to use my talents and great influence." However, forty years of humility and some humiliation broke him to the point where he felt unworthy. He no longer believed that he was the man for the job. He certainly experienced spiritual vertigo.

Moses asked God five questions (they were actually excuses):

1. Who am I? (Exod. 3:11)
2. What if they ask your name? (3:13)
3. What if they will not hear me? (4:1)
4. What if I cannot speak well? (4:10–12)
5. Could you send someone else? (4:13–17)

Moses was indeed a broken man. He was stripped of pride and arrogance. But something stood in the way of his reconciliation with God—himself.

Feelings of guilt about the past can disrupt and cripple our faith. How can God bless us when we fail Him so often? You reason, "God will not bless me; I don't deserve it." Colossians 2:13–14 states, "When you were dead in your transgressions and the uncircumcision of your flesh, He made you alive together with Him, having forgiven us all our transgressions, having canceled out the certificate of debt consisting of decrees against us, which was hostile to us; and He has taken it out of the way, having nailed it to the cross."

Many accept those words as they apply to salvation. We trust that God forgave the sins of our past at the cross.

Our guilt, however, cheapens the cross. We begin to live as if the cross was a down payment for our sins and now we're paying off the balance. We feel we have let God down in the past, so we reason why He would not rescue us in the present. Our spiritual vertigo is often caused by our belief that we are unworthy of His love and grace.

To overcome this, we must realize that the past is past. God can and desires to forgive us. He died to have a relationship with us. So the more pressing issue is: Have you forgiven yourself? Are you approaching God and your relationship with Him with a clear conscience? The Bible says in Hebrews 8:12, "FOR I WILL BE MERCIFUL TO THEIR INIQUITIES, / AND I WILL REMEMBER THEIR SINS NO MORE." If God knows all things and is perfect, how can He forget anything? The idea here is that God will not remember your sins against you any longer.

An example is when someone greatly offends you, and you forgive them and no longer think of their sin when you think of them. You have to be reminded of the wrong they did to you in order to remember it. In the same sense, God no longer thinks of your sin when He thinks of you. He does not hold your sins against you any longer.

Psalm 103:12 states that He has cast our sins "as far as the east is from the west." The east and west never meet. If God forgave us but we can't forgive ourselves, aren't we really saying that we are more righteous than God? We are essentially declaring, "You can forgive me God, but I am a bit too righteous and holy to forgive myself. I must have higher standards than you." However, First John 1:9 says, "If we confess our sins, He is faithful and righteous to forgive us our sins and to cleanse us from all unrighteousness." Have you forgiven yourself with the same grace with which God has forgiven you?

Another reason for feeling unworthy of God's blessings is that we are not following Christ as Lord. Putting it another way, there is sin in our lives. Oftentimes we tolerate sin or wrong attitudes because the world does not cave in on us, so we assume God must be fine with how we live. However, just as we don't get paid every day, we don't necessarily suffer for our sins every day either.

Deep in our hearts, we know the only way to have assurance that God will rescue us is if we follow Him and confess and forsake all our sins. Without this right relationship with Him, our confidence will never come. If we are not following Christ, He cannot afford to bless us. For example, if you're a parent, you know it's poor parenting to give money or privileges to a rebellious child. This only encourages bad behavior. God is not going to bless our bad behavior.

Still another reason we struggle with our past performances is missed opportunities. Performance factors aren't always about committing the negative. Sometimes it's not doing the positive. What is your greatest regret in life? Is it a sin you committed or an opportunity that you missed?

If asked what we would like to "do over" in our life, most of us would recall at least one situation that we regret. The fact that regretful memories come so quickly to our minds is reason enough to believe we haven't let them go. Maybe you feel like God gave you an opportunity to be a Daniel, David, Benaiah or Moses, but you didn't seize it. You feel like you missed your chance. Friend, let it go. No one is perfect. Author Henry Blackaby said it best: "God will do more in six months through a people committed to Him than we could do in sixty years without Him."[1] The door is still open. It's not too late.

Pause right where you are. Pray that God will forgive the sin in your life and bring new opportunities your way as you follow Him.

Other's Performances

Additionally, we're often derailed by the performance of others. Perhaps you're dealing with a rebellious child or a difficult supervisor at work. Can God change them? God is sovereign ruler over all things, but what about free will? Will God change someone as an answer to your prayers?

Moses certainly saw the stubborn people of Israel as an obstacle to God's plans. We read in Exodus 4:1 that Moses asked God, "What if they will not believe me or listen to what I say? For they may say, 'The Lord has not appeared to you.'"

Moses had more bad experiences with the Israelites than he wanted. He remembered Pharaoh chasing him out of Egypt while trying to be their hero. He also remembered being a brave, confident prince when he killed one of the Egyptians to save the life of his Hebrew brethren.

The Hebrews then turned on him. He had to run for his life. So when he remembered his people, the memories were not pleasant ones. I'm sure when he thought of the Israelites, he thought of the life he surrendered to shepherd sheep. If they performed that way before, how could he expect anything different now?

J.P. Moreland and Klaus Issler tell the story of Edith in their book *In Search of a Confident Faith*.

> Edith, now in her early twenties, had experienced significant rejection as a child. She shared her story with Ed Piorek at a ministry conference. "When I was born, I had a twin sister who was stillborn at the same time. I had skeletal formation problems but was otherwise healthy. These problems put a financial strain on my parents. When I was five years old, I was standing outside the kitchen and I heard my father say to my mother, 'I'll never understand it. Why did the one with the perfectly formed body die and the one with the deformities live?' I know my father was speaking out of his frustrations with the challenges of caring for me, but nevertheless it really hurt. I've never been able to forget it."[2]

What about you? Nothing can disappoint you more than people. No one can hurt you more than a person you love. The more you love them, the greater the capacity for hurt. Can God control all things, even people? "If He can't control people," we reason, "He can't control all the circumstances in my life. If He can't control all my circumstances, how can I trust Him? God may mean well. He may love me, but I have to help the situation. I can't just turn it all over to Him, especially if He doesn't have the power to right all things."

The answer is not simple. Yes, God is sovereign. He is so secure in Himself that He can and *has* chosen to give us free will. Yes, He knows the future. He has foreknowledge.

First Peter 1:2 teaches, "according to the foreknowledge of God the Father, by the sanctifying work of the Spirit, to obey

Jesus Christ and be sprinkled with His blood: May grace and peace be yours in the fullest measure." Foreknowledge comes from a Greek word meaning to "know beforehand."[3] When God made promises to us, He knew He could keep them. We can be sure He is sovereign and will keep His promises no matter what it takes.

Will He infringe on the free will of others? No one can really answer that, except to say He will if He wants to—He is God. We'll never be able to answer every question about God. But we do know that we can reconcile what we see, hear and experience.

The Bible says, "The goodness of God leads [people] to repentance" (Rom. 2:4, NKJV). Just know God draws people to Himself through His goodness. This goodness keeps on loving and keeps on giving. God can weave together the wills of people. He can use the hearts and actions of people for His purposes.

Many years ago, *Reader's Digest* ran a story reprinted from *The Jewish Press* entitled "Letter in the Wallet," written by Arnold Fine.

Fine tells the story of finding a wallet with no identification in the street. It contained a few dollars and a sixty-year-old letter addressed to "Michael." The young lady who wrote it was ending their relationship because of her parents, signing, "I will always love you! Hannah." Fine tracked down the now-elderly Hannah to a nursing home.

> When he arrived, a doctor told Fine that Hannah was watching TV in the common room. Fine met with Hannah and explained how he found the letter. "Young man," she said, "This was the last contact I had with Michael. I was only sixteen and my mother forbade us

to see each other anymore. Yes, Michael Goldstein was his name. I loved him very much . . . I never married . . . I guess no one ever matched up to Michael."

As Fine left the home, he told the security guard his story. . . . "Hey, I'd know that wallet anywhere. That's Mr. Goldstein's wallet . . . he's one of the men on the eighth floor." Fine went to the eighth floor, met Mr. Goldstein, and told him that he knew where to find Hannah. "Could you tell me where she is . . . You know, when that letter came to me, my life ended . . . I never stopped loving her."

Fine escorted Michael to see Hannah . . . they embraced . . . three weeks later they were married.[4]

A man and a woman remained true to their first love. God saw fit for the man to drop his wallet at the right time. God sent a trustworthy man to find the wallet and placed a resolve in his heart to find the owner. Fine closed the article by saying, "How good the work of the Lord is." God can work miracles. Remember, Romans 8:28 says, "God causes all things to work together for good."

God's Performance

As I said in the last chapter, our greatest struggles are those we have with God. Many of these struggles revolve around our perception of God's past performances.

Ron Dunn once said that everyone has a secret history with God.[5] People often open up to me and share their stories. Many are heartbreaking. I often wonder how I would feel or react if I were in their shoes, if I struggled to trust God when He doesn't seem to intervene in any tangible way.

Somewhere in our history, most of us feel that God let us down. Our souls cry out for the justification of our spiritual vertigo. How can we trust Him again? The giants in life are very large. What if I'm not the one He picks to bless? One man shared with me an interesting anecdote: "If you woke up tomorrow morning and your spouse had turned into an alligator, you would obviously leap to your feet and run. The alligator then turns back into your wife and promises never to do that again. You would want to believe her, but you would probably always sleep with one eye open."

If you feel like God has let you down before, how can you fully trust Him again? As I mentioned previously, we feel like we deserve better treatment from God. Moses felt like God let him down when he killed the Egyptian. Why follow Him now? Was he going to walk to his death? Was God really going to deliver?

There is an insightful verse in Deuteronomy 8:2 which states, "You shall remember all the way which the LORD your God has led you in the wilderness these forty years, that He might humble you, testing you, to know what was in your heart, whether you would keep His commandments or not." As Moses led Israel out of Egypt, God performed great signs and miracles. Yet the people of Israel rebelled against him and God. Rather than destroy the nation, God allowed them to wander in the wilderness for forty years. He led them through that time of adversity for three reasons:

1. To humble them
2. To test them
3. To know what was in their hearts

Sometimes we need to be humbled. We need to return to the cross. Satan fell because of pride, so it's easy to see how it could be one of his favorite sins. Other times, God gives us trials to test us. With each test passage, we become stronger believers and closer to God.

We've already seen how God places us through brokenness. What else could He do? Have you ever felt like God was nowhere to be found? Ever felt like He was absent in a crisis? That He was silent? There are times when He tests us to reveal what's in our hearts.

At age nineteen, while attending college, I gave my heart anew and afresh to God. It was a passionate, emotional time for me. I reached great heights with God. My excitement grew. I shared my faith with anyone who moved. As one country preacher would often say, "No one was safe." Yet there were times when I became very discouraged, as well. I needed balance.

After two years of this emotional roller coaster, God taught me a valuable lesson. He began to hide Himself from me. He became silent. I experienced no emotional highs. No matter how many times I shared my faith, prayed, worshiped or read my Bible, there was no "pump," no excitement.

That summer, I began to preach quite frequently. I remember the first weeklong revival meeting I preached. It was at my cousin's church, Vineyards Creek Baptist Church, in Comer, Georgia.

It was a great little church. I began preaching that Sunday evening to a packed house of 150 people. I remember worrying all Sunday afternoon. "Is God going to show up? I feel nothing. Will I ever be able to preach? Should I preach?" The service began that evening with an uplifting time of worship, but I had a difficult time participating. I felt spiritually asleep on the inside; but when I stood up to preach, God moved in a wonderful way!

My passion returned. I didn't want to stop preaching. It was the most alive I felt all summer. At the end of the message, I gave a salvation, come-forward style of invitation. When the invitational song began, it seemed God hid Himself from me again. All my emotions subsided. A lady came forward for salvation, but the pastor was already talking to someone else who was making a decision. I reluctantly took the lady by the hand and asked her what decision she was making. She was already crying. The tears of joy filled her eyes as Jesus was filling her heart. I remember vividly saying in my heart to God, "Lord, I wish You would give me some of that." I dealt with the hiddenness of God all summer. When I preached, it was as if God turned on a switch. When I stopped, the switch turned off. I felt like I was fighting for my spiritual life.

Many may think me a hypocrite—I assure you it was no act. I was right with God. I remained faithful. However, the emotional fervor was absent. Why?

I believe He was helping me to discern what was in my heart. During that summer, God gave me a message that I preached for years following. The basic question of the message was "Do you love God, or do you love you and only want God in your life for what He can do for you?" I think the jury was out for me on that question prior to that summer. I found out what was in my heart. I gained maturity in ways I never knew existed.

God's performance is always right. Sometimes He acts, sometimes He is silent, but He is always looking out for our good. He is constructing a deeper relationship of love and faith. With one hand, He humbles us to make us grateful for the past blessings; and with the other, He reaches forward with confidence toward the future. He prepares our hearts and lives to accomplish something wonderful that will magnify Him. He doesn't have to address our every question, our every doubt.

I came to realize that God doesn't answer to me. I answer to Him. He is Lord and I must be grateful for the opportunity to be a part of what He is doing in the world.

Discussion Questions

1. Is there a time in your life where you would like to go back and have a "do-over?" If so, what would that be?
2. Is there someone in your life who is hurting you? If so, how?
3. Can you describe a time when you knew God intervened in your life in a miraculous way? Can you thank God for that right now? How could this affect how you believe God in the future?

5

Dealing with the Dark Side

Our faith will always face opposition. Think with me. Have you ever felt you were in a war but you didn't know what you were fighting? Have you ever fought a battle where you couldn't see the enemy? Where an evil force seemed to be working through friends and acquaintances? Where thoughts found their way into your head to anger you or take you down a dark road of discouragement?

This struggle is what the Bible refers to as spiritual warfare. We face very powerful opposition. Satan is leading this opposition. If you don't believe in spiritual warfare, try to pray silently for five minutes without losing your concentration. You will find your mind starts to wander and a subtle warfare begins to take place.

As I have grown to understand the ways of God, I've found that my greatest personal battles have been with Satan. I feel the warfare when I prepare a sermon. I feel the pressure when I pray or try to minister to someone. When I face spiritual vertigo, I engage in spiritual warfare. Satan is trying to knock me off my spiritual balance.

When we think of the devil, we often think of a little red man with horns and a pitchfork. Those of the Western world generally feel reluctant when they talk about evil and Satan. If a person's head spins around and he vomits all over the place, we might say that it's demonic. Otherwise, we find talk of demons and devils uncomfortable and, at times, offensive.

Mass murders are on the rise in the United States. The past decade has seen an increasing death toll because of them. Included in these are the Sandy Hook School massacre and the slaughter of moviegoers in Aurora, Colorado. We usually place the blame on bad parenting, social rejection and mental illness.

In his book *The Death of Satan*, Andrew Delbanco—a secular liberal—states that our society hates the word "evil" because it places a value judgment on someone else. However, he says, a gulf is opening in our intellectual center enabling us to explain evil in emotional and sociological terms.[1]

In the movie *The Silence of the Lambs*, Officer Clarice Starling meets serial killer Hannibal Lecter for the first time.

Starling: "I think you can provide some insight and advance this study."

Lecter: "And what possible reason could I have to do that?"

Starling: "Curiosity."

Lecter: "About what?"

Starling: "About why you're here. About what happened to you?"

Lecter: "Nothing happened to me, Officer Starling. *I* happened. You can't reduce me to a set of influences. You've given up good and evil for behaviorism, Officer Starling. You've got everyone in moral dignity pants—nothing is ever anybody's fault. Look at me, Officer Starling. Can you stand to say I'm evil? Am I evil, Officer Starling?"[2]

Our society has difficulty answering the monster's question. I challenge you to be consistent in your thinking. Do you believe in a supernatural God? If so, why can't you, in turn, believe in a supernatural evil?

Evil can take more subtle forms than violence and possession. What about discouragement? Anger? Depression? Lack of faith or confidence? Fear? Greed? If you fear the project that God wants you to tackle, if you neglect the Bible, if you feel justified in skipping church services, then you too engage in spiritual warfare.

The more you can't reconcile your faith with your experiences, the more you will engage in spiritual warfare. What greater victory could Satan have than to cause us to doubt our faith?

A passage found in Second Corinthians 4 helps us address this issue: "in whose case the god of this world has blinded the minds of the unbelieving so that they might not see the light of the gospel of the glory of Christ, who is the image of God" (4:4).

The context of this verse comes from one of Paul's more encouraging letters. In it, he reveals a characteristic of Satan. He is powerful enough to blind the minds of people who refuse the gospel. That sounds like a formidable foe. How can we battle this enemy?

Who Do We Fight?

Douglas MacArthur, the great World War II general, said there are four things needed for victory in a war:[3]

1. High morale within the troops
2. Training of personnel
3. An adequate source of supplies
4. Knowledge of the enemy

He goes on to say, "The greater your knowledge of the enemy, the greater your chance of victory."[4]

In Second Corinthians 4:4, what does "god of this world" mean? It means Satan is the god, master and lord over this world's sinful culture. "World" is the idea behind "worldliness" or any lifestyle contrary to the Scriptures. The Bible teaches that God created Satan as a powerful angel:

> "How you have fallen from heaven,
>
> O star of the morning, son of the dawn!
>
> You have been cut down to the earth,
>
> you who have weakened the nations!
>
> "But you said in your heart,
>
> 'I will ascend to heaven;
>
> I will raise my throne above the stars of God,
>
> And I will sit on the mount of assembly
>
> In the recesses of the north.
>
> 'I will ascend above the heights of the clouds;
>
> I will make myself like the Most High.'" (Isa. 14:12–14)

Satan rebelled against God. He wanted to be equal with the Lord. God cast Satan out of heaven along with a third of the angels, who were cohorts in the attempted coup.

The Bible now presents these "fallen angels" as demons. Many of those evil spirits roam the earth today, doing Satan's work.

Satan's main goal is to hurt God by hurting us, His greatest and most loved creation. In John 10:10, Jesus said, "The thief comes only to steal and kill and destroy; I came that they may have life, and have *it* abundantly." Scripture teaches that Satan has great powers which include the following:

Tempting us to sin

And the tempter came and said to Him, 'If You are the Son of God, command that these stones become bread (Matt. 4:3).

Stealing the Word from our hearts

When anyone hears the word of the kingdom and does not understand it, the evil one comes and snatches away what has been sown in his heart. This is the one on whom seed was sown beside the road (Matt. 13:19).

Making us feel guilty for our forgiven sins

Then I heard a loud voice in heaven, saying, 'Now the salvation, and the power, and the kingdom of our God and the authority of His Christ have come, for the accuser of our brethren has been thrown down, he who accuses them before our God day and night'(Rev. 12:10).

Delaying an answer to prayer

Then he said to me, 'Do not be afraid, Daniel, for from the first day that you set your heart on understanding this and on humbling yourself before your God, your words were heard, and I have come in response to your words. But the prince of the kingdom of Persia was withstanding me for twenty-one days; then behold, Michael, one of the chief princes, came to help me, for I had been left there with the kings of Persia' (Dan. 10:12–13; Note: This Persian prince is a demonic force).[5]

Developing strongholds or sinful habits in our lives

For the weapons of our warfare are not of the flesh, but divinely powerful for the destruction of fortresses. We are destroying speculations and every lofty thing raised up against the knowledge of God, and we are taking every thought captive to the obedience of Christ (2 Cor. 10:4–5).

Destroying lives

The thief comes only to steal and kill and destroy; I came that they may have life, and have it abundantly (John 10:10).

Blinding the minds of unbelievers

In whose case the god of this world has blinded the minds of the unbelieving so that they might not see the light of the gospel of the glory of Christ, who is the image of God (2 Cor. 4:4).

This type of blindness comes from a Greek word *agnosia*, meaning "an inability to understand or comprehend truth."[6] The battleground for the fight is our mind. Proverbs 23:7 states, "For as he thinks within himself, so he is."

If you could place your thoughts into a person's mind so they receive your thoughts as their own, you could lead their choices. In some cases, you could even rule their lives.

Adolph Hitler knew this. That's why taking over the school system in Germany was vital to the plans of the Third Reich.

The ideals of Karl Marx infiltrated the minds of influential, radical people and, through communism, enslaved millions. Satan has used this battle plan since God cast him out of heaven.

Looking again at Second Corinthians 4:4, the word "unbelieving" refers to a person's conscious choice to reject God's Word.[7]

Why would someone do that? Jesus taught in John 3:19–20, "This is the judgment, that the Light has come into the world, and men loved the darkness rather than the Light, for their deeds were evil. For everyone who does evil hates the Light, and does not come to the Light for fear that his deeds will be exposed."

The late Chuck Colson used to tell a story about when he had dinner with talk-show host Larry King. Although King is not a professed Christian, he has interviewed many notable Christian ministers such as Colson, Rick Warren and Billy Graham, and has given them a fair hearing.

As they met for dinner, King looked at Colson over the table and said, "I'm going to give you two hours to convince me that Jesus Christ is Savior, Lord and King." After two hours of stating the case for Christ, King replied, "I am not convinced." Colson replied, "I don't believe you want to be convinced." King replied, "You are right."[8]

What happens when the Word of God speaks to our minds and hearts? The Bible says we either accept or reject it. If we accept it, then God enlightens us with knowledge of Him. If we reject the Word, even what we know and comprehend departs from us eventually (see the parable of the sower in Matthew 13).

An analysis of our enemy reveals there is a limit to Satan's power. He influences us toward evil, but he can't make us do anything. He is, however, powerful enough to place his thoughts inside our heads and bring us to a point where we doubt God and His Word. There may never be another Adolph Hitler, but thoughts can easily result in discouraged hearts, negative attitudes and wrong decisions.

We must be careful to whom and what we listen. A word from Satan can take human form. It could be a teacher treating you as if you're "stupid." It could be the discouraging words of a parent. It could even be your own imagination. Second Corinthians 10:5 (KJV) teaches, "Casting down imaginations, and every high thing that exalteth itself against the knowledge of God, and bringing into captivity every thought to the obedience of Christ."

If you're like me, you're often lost in your thoughts. We often talk to ourselves as our imaginations run wild. Sometimes these thoughts and speculations lead down dark paths. We not only talk to ourselves, but we also listen to the answers, which may have a negative and depressing nature. This begs the question, "Are these thoughts our own or are they placed there by Satan?"

In his book *I Talk Back to the Devil*, A.W. Tozer believes many such thoughts are from Satan. He says we must give him back talk to defend ourselves. We must reject his lies. These thoughts are forms of temptation.[9] Talk back to him when he suggests thoughts like, "Although God blesses some, He won't bless me." Don't listen. He's tempting you to doubt God. When you feel paralyzed with fear and can't move forward with God's vision, talk back. The devil's trying to ruin your future by telling you that God can't be trusted. Our mind is Satan's battleground because we have thousands of thoughts a day. It's easy to see what we're facing.

To win in this life, we must recognize our enemy. I didn't serve in the Vietnam War, but I had friends and coworkers who fought valiantly. I asked them, "What was the most difficult part of fighting the war?" Virtually all of them mentioned they couldn't clearly identify the enemy because North and South Vietnamese people looked, talked and dressed the same. It is also sometimes difficult for us to identify our spiritual enemy. Just like the North and South Vietnamese looked the same to the soldiers, without proper training, good and evil can also "look" the same to us.

If the Bible is correct about spiritual warfare—and it is—our own resources will never be enough to overcome the darkness within our hearts, families, relationships or world. We need the supernatural to battle the supernatural. We need Christ.

What Do We Fight?

What are we facing? What is Satan's ammunition? In Ephesians 6:10–11, Paul warns us about the enemy: "Finally, be strong in the Lord and in the strength of His might. Put on the full armor of God, so that you will be able to stand firm against the schemes of the devil." Notice the key word: *schemes*! It comes from the Greek word *methodeia*, meaning "wiles, methods or strategies."[10] Second Corinthians 2:11 teaches, "No advantage would be taken of us by Satan, for we are not ignorant of his schemes."

Another key word is "wrestling." Ephesians 6:12 (kjv) says, "For we wrestle not against flesh and blood, but against principalities, against powers, against the rulers of the darkness of this world, against spiritual wickedness in high places." This word implies an intense battle. Literally, it means "hands or knuckles on the ground."[11] This verse also speaks of the rulers of a force of darkness in the world. These are powerful words. Paul exposes our dangerous foe. We must not take him lightly.

What Does Satan Do?

To understand the schemes of the devil, the key is in the word: *devil*. It means "liar or slanderer."[12] Again, the mind is a battlefield and lies are his ammunition.

In his book, *All Marketers Are Liars*, author Seth Godin writes that we all tell stories in our own minds. We convince ourselves these stories are true and reject opposition, even to the point of anger.[13] His example shows that most conservatives watch Fox News while liberals may watch CNN. We all want confirmation of our own beliefs, so we interact with people who affirm our views.

In my early years as a pastor, a woman from our community disagreed with me on a scriptural issue. She considered herself an activist and was involved in civic and social issues. One day, while speaking to her husband, we agreed to come together for a discussion.

I decided to bring along another minister from the church. She seemed to like him, so I thought it would be a good idea. But the moment we walked in the house, she met me with great resistance. She didn't approve that I spoke with her husband first, nor did she like that I brought a witness.

Not long into our conversation, I realized she'd made up her mind with her own story. I truthfully answered each question and explained my position. But she told me I wasn't being honest with her. No matter what I said, if it didn't match her story, she believed I was lying.

Since that day, more than twenty years ago, I've had many conversations with folks convinced they knew the real story, but they only had a small percentage of the facts. I wonder how many of those stories came from Satan, who attacks our minds with lies.

How many of our "what ifs" come from him? How many of our "I betchas" come from him? "I betcha" he stole that; "I betcha" he said that about me; "I betcha" that man has a hidden agenda. Our thoughts and stories don't all originate with us.

How Does Satan Do It?

Satan has many strategies. The two most common are temptation and accusation. Both are attacks on our self-centeredness.

When I'm tempted, I think too highly of myself. I convince myself to do what I know I shouldn't do. I think, "I am the exception. I can always receive forgiveness later. After all, I'm under grace." When Satan met Eve in Eden, he said, "You surely will not die! For God knows that in the day you eat from it your eyes will be opened, and you will be like God, knowing good and evil" (Gen. 3:4–5). What Satan really told Eve was, "God's trying to cheat you." He uses that same method today to convince us God is trying to cheat us out of a good time, happiness, pleasure, prosperity, money . . . being our own boss. Satan tempts you, telling you that you deserve what God forbids.

His second strategy is accusation. Revelation 12:10 teaches, "Now the salvation, and the power, and the kingdom of our God and the authority of His Christ have come, for the accuser of our brethren has been thrown down, he who accuses them before our God day and night." When accused, I think less of myself. Satan tells me I don't deserve forgiveness or God's love. He says, "God loves everyone; but *you*, not so much. You aren't privileged. You're not an overcomer. God will never forgive you."

In Part 4 of his blog series: "The World, the Flesh and the Devil," musician and speaker Shaun Groves writes how Satan "plays" Christians by comparing the mechanics of a piano to our mind. Classified as a percussion instrument, the piano's keys must strike its strings to produce a sound. But that's not the truth.

A piano will play without even being touched. Just open the lid of a grand piano, lean over its strings and sing. Somewhere in the network of strings, you'll find one that vibrates, tuned to the frequency of the note you sing. Stop singing and the string goes on vibrating, singing your note back to you. Groves explains how Satan uses the same principle to plant lies in our minds, "He leans in close, hovers over the strings of my flesh, and sings his lies. And the flesh buzzes, reverberates gladly and sin sings forth." When this happens, Satan is playing you![14]

How Do We Fight Satan?

Remember, General MacArthur said one of the four things needed to win a battle is adequate resources. We need proper weapons to fight a spiritual battle. In his second letter to the church of Corinth, Paul wrote, "For though we walk in the flesh, we do not war according to the flesh, for the weapons of our warfare are not of the flesh, but divinely powerful for the destruction of fortresses. *We are* destroying speculations and every lofty thing raised up against the knowledge of God, and *we are* taking every thought captive to the obedience of Christ" (2 Cor. 10:3–5). We live in a physical world. However, many of our battles are spiritual and our weapons must therefore be spiritual.

In Ephesians 6:10–17, Paul also writes about the weapons used for spiritual warfare.

> Finally, be strong in the Lord and in the strength of His might. Put on the full armor of God, so that you will be able to stand firm against the schemes of the devil. For our struggle is not against flesh and blood, but against the rulers, against the powers, against the world forces of this darkness, against the spiritual *forces* of wickedness in the heavenly *places*. Therefore, take up the full armor of God, so that you will be able to resist in the evil day, and having done everything, to stand

firm. Stand firm therefore, *having girded your loins with truth* and *having put on the breastplate of righteousness*, and having shod *your feet with the preparation of the gospel of peace*; in addition to all, taking up the shield of faith with which you will be able to extinguish all the flaming arrows of the evil *one*. And take *the helmet of salvation* and the sword of the Spirit, which is the Word of God.

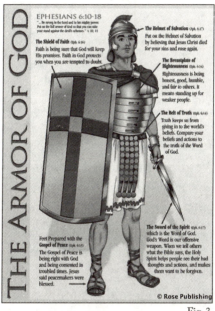

Fig. 3.

Paul wrote his letter to the church at Ephesus while in a Roman prison. During his first Roman imprisonment, the Roman guards wore suits of armor, similar to that which is shown in figure 3.[15]

I imagine Paul trying to describe the spiritual warfare that believers experience. Looking at the Roman armor, he drew analogies to all the spiritual weapons we possess. He described the importance of these weapons which enable us to stand firm in our faith.

Paul used the phrase "stand firm" three times in Ephesians 6:11–14. He wanted us to prepare ourselves against the constant attacks of Satan, who tries to discourage us, drive us away from faith and closeness to God, procrastinate our actions, yield to old temptations, doubt and quit. An army that takes a hill in battle needs to have the resources and strength to occupy what they conquer.

To do that, we must use the weapons of God. In Ephesians 6:14, Paul tells us the belt of truth is our defense against deception. It holds the armor together. The soldier even tucked his tunic into his belt while he ran. Truth holds everything together. We fend off false teaching, discouraging thoughts, negative attitudes, lies and speculation because we believe, embrace and apply God's Word. Truth matters! If we don't operate by the truth, we operate at a great disadvantage in life. This is true in science and mathematics as well as in spiritual matters.

Next, Paul said, put on the breastplate of righteousness. Living right guards our spiritual heart, but sin hardens the heart against God. It causes us to reject God's Word.

Then, Paul labeled the soldier's footwear as the gospel of peace. Roman soldiers wore sandals with spiked soles, fundamental to security in rough terrain.[16] The good news Jesus unveiled at the cross, the gospel of peace, is foundational to winning battles. A person with inner turmoil cannot hope to be at his best in spiritual battle. It's from a base of peace that we are free from guilt to battle with a clear conscience.

Paul then introduced the shield of faith. Extending four by two feet, the shield's flexibility made it the soldier's best defensive weapon against the enemy's attack.[17] Faith means believing that God exists, but it also means believing He rewards those who seek Him (see Heb. 11:6). It is the belief that, although evidence may insinuate that God is guilty of being unrewarding, all the evidence has yet to be presented. Faith is the belief we're better off trusting God than following the schemes of Satan.

Paul spoke of the helmet of salvation. A helmet protects the head. To keep the faith, our salvation is foundational, so we must guard our minds until the conclusion of our salvation in heaven.

The final weapon mentioned, the sword of the Spirit, was the only offensive weapon on Paul's list. This is the Word of God. When Jesus was in the wilderness (see Matt. 4), He used Scripture three times to combat Satan's temptations. Scripture is a powerful weapon in our arsenal.

A friend of mine tells a story of a time God used the Word of God to help him resist temptation. As a private in the Army and out of the country for the first time, he found himself getting lonely. One evening while on leave, he yielded to temptation and followed his fellow soldiers to a bar. Leaving the bar, the soldiers decided to visit a nearby brothel. His heart was torn because he knew going into this establishment would surely lead him to sin and down a dark, dangerous path.

Surrendering to the temptation, he joined them. At the door, each of them was happily greeted by the madam until it was his turn. When she came to him, she stopped, looked into his eyes, and quoted Galatians 6:7, "Do not be deceived, God is not mocked; for whatever a man sows, this he will also reap."

How could she know that he was a believer? How did she know that verse of Scripture? My friend turned, left the house, and returned to his barracks. After his time of military service, he returned to the states, and eventually served as a pastor for many years.

The Word of God—so powerful. It saved the ministry, and perhaps the life, of a future pastor.

Knowing and applying the Word of God saved a great pastor's ministry. It's a powerful weapon for us as well.

Although not mentioned in the armor illustration, we find a great weapon in prayer. Ephesians 6:18 says, "With all prayer and petition pray at all times in the Spirit, and with this in view, be on the alert with all perseverance and petition for all the saints."

We pray with thanksgiving. Again, gratitude connects our past and future with faith. In addition, we must pray for God's strength, protection and intervention in our problems. Prayer is vital to living in victory. In Exodus 17, we read the story of a battle fought at Rephidim between the nations of Israel and Amalek. It serves as a fitting illustration.

> Then Amalek came and fought against Israel at Rephidim. So Moses said to Joshua, "Choose men for us and go out, fight against Amalek. Tomorrow I will station myself on the top of the hill with the staff of God in my hand." Joshua did as Moses told him, and fought against Amalek; and Moses, Aaron, and Hur went up to the top of the hill. So it came about when Moses held his hand up, that Israel prevailed, and when he let his hand down, Amalek prevailed. But Moses' hands were heavy. Then they took a stone and put it under him, and he sat on it; and Aaron and Hur supported his hands, one on one side and one on the other. Thus his hands were steady until the sun set. So Joshua overwhelmed

Amalek and his people with the edge of the sword.
(Ex. 17:8–13)

As you read this story, notice that Joshua was winning every time Moses raised his arms in intervention toward heaven. When Moses grew tired and dropped his arms, Amalek turned the tide. Finally, two men held Moses' arms up and the Israelites won the battle. Though Joshua received most of the credit, we know the whole story. Moses' prayers moved God to fight for His people.

The Bible calls us to be consistent, prevailing and passionate in our prayer. Psalm 55:17 (NLT) teaches, "Morning, noon, and night / I cry out in my distress, / and the LORD hears my voice." Jeremiah 33:3 says, "Call to Me and I will answer you, and I will tell you great and mighty things, which you do not know." Here, the word "call" gives the impression of crying out in fervency, passion and desperation to God.

I admit my prayers are more like counseling sessions with God. I often find myself relaxed when talking to God as though I am talking to a friend. There are times when this is good. But I found until I began crying out to God (sometimes to the point of fasting) I didn't receive the answers I needed.

A few years ago, when going through the challenges I mentioned previously, I remember being desperate for an answer my prayers. Convicted by God, I fasted for twenty-one days. During this time, not only did I draw closer to God, but I also learned to cry out to Him. In those twenty-one days, I prayed for answers to seven requests . . . and God answered all of them. I'm not claiming that by fasting and crying out in prayer, God will somehow turn into a supernatural genie. I'm simply saying God comes to our defense when we use His weapons in battle.

Why Must We Battle?

Battle is necessary. Muscles build through resistance. We develop character through adversity. Remember, however, we must operate from a place of victory. Hebrews 2:14 teaches, "Therefore, since the children share in flesh and blood, He Himself likewise also partook of the same, that through death He might render powerless him who had the power of death, that is, the devil." Spiritual vertigo is simply a deception. Our faith can't process what we see, hear or experience because we believe things that aren't true. We believe what *we* think is best for our lives. We feel like God is trying to cheat us or that He has favorites. We might even believe we're not worthy. We think because God didn't come through before, He can't be fully trusted.

We are engaged in spiritual warfare, fighting for our faith. We overcome it by coming to the cross daily in humility, maintaining a close relationship with God, and feeding ourselves with the Word.

Let me close this chapter with a simple story. There is a tale of an Eskimo who lived in the hills of Alaska. Every Saturday, he came down the mountain with his two dogs, one white and one black. The dogs fought and many of the townspeople bet on which would win (I don't advocate this).

Sometimes the white dog won and other times the black dog won, but each time the old Eskimo won the bet. One Saturday, a young man in town followed the Eskimo back to his home. He asked the Eskimo, "Sometimes the white dog wins and sometimes the black dog wins, but you always win! How do you know which dog will win?" The Eskimo replied, "That's easy. It's whichever one I feed the most."

When light and darkness battle for our faith, which one will win? The one we feed the most.

Discussion Questions

1. What is Satan's role versus your role in temptation? (See James 1:13–15)
2. Why do you think we avoid talking about Satan and spiritual warfare?
3. Where do you find spiritual warfare most apparent in your life?
4. How can you feed your "good dog" (spiritual side) more than your "bad dog" (fleshly side)?

6

Embracing the Truth

So faith comes *from hearing, and
hearing by the word of Christ.*

Romans 10:17

Why do we have problems trusting God? Why do we have problems with spiritual vertigo? Why can't we just move forward and accomplish great things in our lives?

We trust people based on what we know about them. We base our response on whether or not we believe what they say. In a world of contracts, lawyers, lawsuits and loopholes, commitment seems temporary. Because of this, we tend to see God in the same light.

But His Word is His bond. The key to trust is taking God at His Word, which is the Bible and our source of faith. It's our spiritual food source. We come to know God's character—His attitude, His heart—all because of the Bible. If it were not for the Scriptures, we'd never know salvation or growth in Christ. We wouldn't know God.

The Bible says the best way to grow in faith is through hearing, reading, studying and applying Scripture. But do we really believe the Bible? Do we live as though we believe it?

Could it be that while we're in the trenches, we can't believe God because we never came to terms with His Word?

To transition from "no longer" to "not yet," we must trust and follow His Word.

The Problem

In Second Peter 1:16–21, we find one of the New Testament passages concerning Scripture. Peter wrote this letter to encourage believers during times of adversity. He warned them not to fall into the hands of false teachers. Later he taught about the second coming of Christ and signs of the end times. But here, in Second Peter 1:12, he told believers, "Therefore, I will always be ready to remind you of these things, even though you *already* know *them*, and have been established in the truth which is present with *you*."

Peter said, as long as he was alive, he would remind them of what's important and needful. In Second Peter 1:16-21, he wrote about one of these needful things—Scripture. In verse 19 he reiterated, "So we have the prophetic word *made* more sure, to which you do well to pay attention as to a lamp shining in a dark place, until the day dawns and the morning star arises in your hearts."

Do you see the connection between Scripture and spiritual vertigo? We must pay attention to God's Word. It's like a lamp shining in murky waters. There are times we go through dark, lonely places with nowhere to turn—undesirous of God's will when the answers to prayer don't come, when the presence of God seems far away, when God seems silent. It is in these times we need Him most. It is during these dark times that His Word will shine a heavenly light into our lives.

In Scripture, light symbolizes several key elements to our faith. We find that light represents knowledge. The Bible often gives our hearts great comfort and insight during tough times. A few years ago, I experienced a very dark time. Looking back, I felt under attack and wondered when it would end. God led me to Isaiah 54:15–17.

> If anyone fiercely assails *you* it will not be from Me.
> Whoever assails you will fall because of you.
> Behold, I Myself have created the smith who blows
> the fire of coals
> And brings out a weapon for its work;
> And I have created the destroyer to ruin.
> No weapon that is formed against you will prosper;
> And every tongue that accuses you in judgment you
> will condemn.
> This is the heritage of the servants of the LORD,
> And their vindication is from Me," declares the LORD.

These verses spoke to me and I felt the light of God encourage me. His assurance was present, even in the dark.

Light represents hope. Some of the most popular television pastors in America are dispensers of hope. Many of these preachers may lack scriptural depth or disregard the Bible completely. So why do so many flock to hear them preach? They bring hope to the hearer. But without scriptural trust, hope is empty. It's not enough to have man-made light. We must allow the Word to shine truth and hope into our hearts.

Light speaks to wisdom. Romans 10:17 says, "So faith *comes* from hearing, and hearing by the word of Christ." As I read the Bible, my faith builds. The more I know God, the easier it is to trust Him. This has application in all relationships. To trust someone, we must know them. The more trustworthy a person proves to be, the easier it is to trust them.

Light also builds supernatural insight within us. The Bible inspires; and the Holy Spirit uses it supernaturally to build our bold faith which leads us to make courageous decisions, to hang tough in troubled times, to seize new opportunities assured of God's presence. We take the initiative in ministry, sensing God's presence and power in our lives.

So what's the problem? Don't we really believe in the Bible enough to trust it? For example, in John 14:6, one of the most controversial Bible verses, Jesus proclaimed, "I am the way, and the truth, and the life; no one comes to the Father but through Me."

Fifty-seven percent of evangelical church members truly believe there are other ways to heaven.[1] The church now follows the culture's example on defining and raising a family, social, and ethical issues, and practical living. It appears there's little difference between how the world (those not following Christ) and the church live today.

When faced with social or cultural issues, modern Christians seem to side with the culture, while questioning or simply ignoring Bible truth. Questions abound, like "Did Jesus ever speak about that?" Comments like "the Bible seldom speaks about that issue in the New Testament" are frequent.

I often hear this question from committed believers, "I wonder if I could die for my faith?" In college, my good friend Kevin took a summer mission trip to Turkey. He traveled with a mission organization called Operation Mobilization, which often took college students to distribute literature in countries closed to the gospel. Kevin and his small team drove through the streets of a city (much like a UPS driver) and dropped study materials at front doors while people slept. One night, the police stopped their van, found the literature and arrested them.

Kevin said they sang while in prison (like Paul and Silas) until told to "shut up." Looking first at the faces of the police officers and then at their guns, it suddenly struck them they'd spread the gospel in a Muslim country. They might die that night!

He said, "I didn't know if I was really ready. Could I do it?" God eventually intervened and they were released. But the question deserves reflection.

It bears thought, especially when you consider that many American Christians deny scriptural truth in order to blend with culture. How could we *die* for Him if we can't even *stand* for Him? We all seek acceptance. No one wants to be persecuted or ostracized from a group. We want others to think us tolerant and accepting. But what priority does the Bible really have in your life?

When we deny biblical truth, it negatively affects our ability to trust. We aren't built for a dualistic mind-set. Our courage erodes and our spiritual struggle intensifies when we doubt God and His Word on significant issues. Subconsciously, we have difficulty believing any of the Bible when we deny parts of it. When we experience a dark time, doubt becomes our first reaction.

Sometimes it seems we treat God's Word like a stranger. In Old Testament times, homes were always (temporarily) open to strangers. But they never became part of the family. They were just visitors, and the family never got involved in their lives. We often treat God's Word in this way. We invite the Bible into our lives, but we do not allow it to affect our lives.

From the beginning, Satan's methods cast doubt on God's Word.

> Now the serpent was more crafty than any beast of the field which the LORD God had made. And he said to the woman, "Indeed, has God said, 'You shall not eat from any tree of the garden'?" The woman said to the serpent, "From the fruit of the trees of the garden we may eat; but from the fruit of the tree which is in the middle of the garden, God has said 'You shall not eat from it or touch it, or you will die.'" The serpent said to the woman, "You surely will not die! For God knows that in the day you eat from it your eyes will be opened, and you will be like God, knowing good and evil." When the woman saw that the tree was good for food, and that it was a delight to the eyes, and that the tree was desirable to make *one* wise, she took from its fruit and ate; and she gave also to her husband with her, and he ate. (Gen. 3:1-6)

Satan's first step cast doubt on what God said. Then, he denied God's Word—"You surely will not die!" Finally, he substituted God's Word: "For God knows that in the day you eat from it your eyes will be opened, and you will be like God, knowing good and evil" (Gen. 3:5). Today, Satan attacks us with the same methods he used with Eve thousands of years ago.

We're also inclined to be selective with Scripture, choosing to believe what fits our lifestyle. For example, two young men interviewed a third as a potential roommate. They told him they were Christians. However, their lifestyle didn't match what they said they believed. They said they were trying to get as many girls as possible to sleep with them. Hasn't the Bible spoken to this already?

Though this example may be extreme, we often take a similar approach to Scripture. Do you know how God wants you to handle money? Do you know what He says about church attendance and involvement? Hebrews 10:25 teaches, "not forsaking our own assembling together, as is the habit of some, but encouraging *one another*, and all the more as you see the day drawing near." Do you know what Scripture says about serving others? Placing others before yourself? Helping the poor? My point is that we will struggle with God until we believe, trust and obey all of His Word. We'll find it difficult to believe Him in the dark times. Only when God's Word is our final life authority will we be able to trust Him in the tough times. It's then that we place ourselves on the path to spiritual balance.

Can I Trust the Bible?

Second Peter 1:16–21 presents six very persuasive arguments that offer evidence of biblical truth.

> For we did not follow cleverly devised tales when we made known to you the power and coming of our Lord Jesus Christ, but we were eyewitnesses of His majesty. For when He received honor and glory from God the Father, such an utterance as this was made to Him by the Majestic Glory, "This is My beloved Son with whom I am well-pleased"—and we ourselves heard this utterance made from heaven when we were with Him on the holy mountain.
>
> *So* we have the prophetic word *made* more sure, to which you do well to pay attention as to a lamp shining in a dark place, until the day dawns and the morning star arises in your hearts. But know this first of all, that no prophecy of Scripture is *a matter* of one's own

> interpretation, for no prophecy was ever made by an
> act of human will, but men moved by the Holy Spirit
> spoke from God.

Notice the reliability of biblical history mentioned in Second Peter 1:16 where it says, "For we did not follow cleverly devised tales when we made known to you the power and coming of our Lord Jesus Christ, but we were eyewitnesses of His majesty." Peter is saying that the Scriptures are not tales or mere fiction. These were eyewitness accounts. Some would protest, citing the lack of original biblical manuscripts (which, if we had, would be worshiped, as is much of God's creation).

Keep in mind, we have 24,000 copies of New Testament manuscripts or fragments and 14,000 Old Testament documents.[2] When we compare that to other ancient documents, the Bible fares well. As an example, 643 manuscripts exist of Homer's *Iliad*, but no one questions its authenticity. We can only locate 49 Aristotle manuscripts and 7 for Plato, but who questions them?

Part of Israel's calling as a nation was to preserve God's Word. They meticulously copied these manuscripts. Paul said of the Scriptures in Second Timothy 3:16, "All Scripture is inspired by God and profitable for teaching, for reproof, for correction, for training in righteousness." "All" means every Scripture. The word inspiration comes from the Greek word *theopneustos*, meaning "God-breathed."[3] Paul believed all Scripture was the Word or breath of God. Since God cannot breathe error, we know what God said is perfect and true. Psalm 119:89 says, "Forever, O Lord, / Your word is settled in heaven."

Sir William Ramsay said, "The Bible writers were first rate and should be placed among the greatest historians that ever lived."[4] Josephus, a first-century Roman historian, confirmed many of the New Testament writers' claims: including the death, burial and resurrection of Christ.

Archeology has also confirmed the Bible. Digging up old ruins might seem a bit boring, (although the *Indiana Jones* films may have changed our perceptions) but archeology is important. We research our past through this discipline to determine whether our beliefs, lifestyle and faith are grounded in objective truth.

As a student at Southwestern Theological Seminary, I saw many artifacts in a special room dedicated to the results of archeological diggings. This room is evidence of the many tribes that were alive during biblical times. Historian Nelson Glueck said, "It may be stated categorically that no archeological discovery has ever controverted a biblical reference."[5]

In Second Peter 1:16–19, we also find writers who were "eyewitnesses" in the presence of other "eyewitnesses." Here, Peter recalls the time he, James and John were with Jesus on the Mount of Transfiguration when Moses and Elijah descended from heaven. "For we did not follow cleverly devised tales when we made known to you the power and coming of our Lord Jesus Christ, but we were eyewitnesses of His majesty." These were clearly not devised (concocted) tales, said Peter. The closer the eyewitness, the more accurate the account. They were there when it happened.

I once read about a group of people who believed the Holocaust was a hoax. They said the Jewish people in Hollywood made it up to gain sympathy for the Jewish race. But eyewitness accounts tell of prisons like Auschwitz, the gas chambers, and written documentation detailing how people were convinced to march to their death without a shot fired. It's vital to note these eyewitness accounts were conveyed and written during the lifetimes of other eyewitnesses.

A few years ago, I was privileged to play in the Open Championship in Scotland. It was a difficult course to play under windy conditions, but I prevailed and they placed my name on the famous Claret Jug. Commentators still talk about my final round as being one of the greatest in any major tournament. I'll never forget my final putt on the eighteenth hole and how it felt as the ball trickled into the cup. What a great feeling to win the 2013 Open Championship! "Wait a minute!" you say. "Are you claiming to have won the 2013 Open? That's a lie! I watched it on television. A friend of mine was there for all four rounds! Phil Mickelson won that tournament. I don't recall you even playing!"

Busted! You're right. I didn't play in that tournament, much less win. You see, if I tell an untrue story in the presence of eyewitnesses, they expose my lie. First-century eyewitnesses would have exposed the resurrection and other claims of the apostles had they been untrue.

Peter witnessed Jesus' performance of miracles. He walked on the water with Jesus. He prayed with Jesus on the Mount of Transfiguration, witnessed Jesus' death on the cross for our sins and saw Jesus' resurrected body. These accounts were verified by other eyewitnesses. The Bible tells us that, in one sighting alone, more than five hundred people witnessed Jesus alive after the resurrection. Many of these people were still living during the writing of the New Testament.

The evidence of scriptural truth is in its supernatural events. There were many biblical miracles, but the greatest event in history was the resurrection of Jesus Christ. It's also the greatest proof for Christianity. The entirety of Christianity is based on three things:

1. A person (Christ)
2. A book (the Bible)
3. An event (the resurrection of Christ)

People debate the claims of Christ, but here are ten things we know about Jesus from secular history:

1. He died by means of crucifixion on a Roman cross.
2. His body was placed in a guarded tomb.
3. The apostles were shattered that their Messiah had died. They lost all hope without expectation of a resurrection.
4. His tomb was found empty on the third day.
5. Eyewitnesses reported the bodily appearance of Jesus on several occasions.
6. The apostles' shattered faith radically transformed into bold belief in the resurrection. They were willing to sacrifice their lives for this belief.
7. The early church proclamation was unapologetically the resurrection of Christ.
8. The Christian church sprang from news of the resurrection. Sunday became the day of worship.
9. Jesus appeared to James and Paul, who experienced conversion.
10. The body of Jesus was never found.

From historical accounts outside of the Bible, we know the tomb was empty. The biggest question is, "Did Jesus rise from the dead?" Many theories over the years have tried to disprove the resurrection. For instance, the "swoon theory" of 1828 implies that Jesus survived the following: thirty-nine stripes from a whip called the cat-o'-nine-tails, six hours nailed to a cross, a Roman spear thrust in His side, the pronunciation of death by two Roman executioners and being wrapped up like a mummy for three days.

It also suggests that He had enough strength to roll away a one- to two-ton stone, sneak past the Roman guards, and appear clean and unwounded before His disciples.[6] This is simply not a believable theory.

Then there is the "hallucination theory." This theory claims the women at the tomb hallucinated when they claimed to have seen Jesus.[7] I guess the Roman guards, apostles and five hundred witnesses also hallucinated. Not very plausible.

The only real possibilities are that Jesus' body was stolen or that He rose from the dead. If His body was stolen, who did it—His enemies or His friends?

If His enemies stole the body, why didn't they later produce the body? The Jewish leaders had only to show everyone the body of Christ, squelching the credibility of the apostles, and the Christianity movement would have been finished. But the body was never produced.

What about his friends? Unlike the Jewish leaders, the apostles had no opportunity. The Jewish leaders remembered Jesus' prophecy about His resurrection, so at their insistence, the Romans stationed soldiers at the tomb. The Jewish leaders prepared for the disciples to try to steal the body. The claim that somehow the guards went to sleep would be highly unlikely; they were professionals, and going to sleep on guard duty would be punishable by death.

I also argue that the disciples had no motive. They didn't see the resurrection coming. At the arrest of Jesus, they ran for their lives. The picture here is one of disillusionment, despair and fear. If these men stole the body, why did they die for an empty cause? Arguably, many died for their faith, but they believed they were dying for something true. The problem here is that if the disciples stole the body, they died for something they knew was a lie.[8]

Look at what happened to the disciples.

- Matthew was killed in Ethiopia.
- Peter, Simon, Andrew, and Philip were crucified.
- James and Paul were beheaded.
- Thomas was pierced with a lance.
- James the Lesser was stoned to death.[9]

Sir Lionel Luckhoo, a highly successful trial attorney with 245 consecutive murder acquittals said, "I say unequivocally the evidence for the resurrection of Jesus Christ is so overwhelming that it compels acceptance by proof which leaves absolutely no room for doubt."[10]

Fulfilled prophecy is evidence of biblical authority and truth. No other religion has predictive prophecy. More than two thousand predictive prophecies in the Old Testament were fulfilled in the New Testament. These included the birth of Jesus Christ (both its origin and place), His death and His resurrection. There are hundreds of prophecies in the New Testament predicting the second coming of Christ. Signs and prophecies including a drastic increase in knowledge, earthquakes, famine, drug use (see Rev. 9), Israel's nationhood and a falling away from the faith, just to list a few.

Several years ago, a tract society produced a yellow newspaper entitled *Jesus Comes Again*. They wrote the paper as though the rapture—the taking away of believers—had occurred the day before. The articles described stories of plane crashes, car accidents and missing babies. The paper also listed the biblical signs leading up to the second coming. A friend of mine gave one of the newspapers to some coworkers. The newspaper articles sounded so similar to what was actually happening around them that one guy looked up, pale-faced, and said, "Man, this is scaring me to death!"

The Source of Scripture

The Bible claims God, not man, as its source, which leads to the biggest question: Is the Bible from God? Second Peter 1:20–21 says, "But know this first of all, that no prophecy of Scripture is a *matter* of one's own interpretation, for no prophecy was ever made by an act of human will, but men moved by the Holy Spirit spoke from God."

It says the men were "moved" to write. The word "moved" comes from the Greek word meaning "to steer" (like a ship's rudder). Some argue that if the men were only inspired, then there could be mistakes. However, it doesn't say they were inspired. It says they were steered. Again, Second Timothy 3:16 testifies, "All Scripture is inspired by God and profitable for teaching, for reproof, for correction, for training in righteousness."

This verse states the Scriptures themselves were inspired or God-breathed. The writers moved under God's direction and the Bible itself is God's Word to us. This means the individual writers and their personalities were woven into Scriptures. I'm grateful for this because exact scriptural replicas would bring suspicion that the writers copied from one another. Of course, the main proof of Scripture is that it survives centuries of bad sermons!

The Importance of Understanding Scriptural Integrity

If we don't believe the Bible is God's Word, we won't trust it. Not trusting the Bible will make it difficult to know God. All we objectively know about God is from the Bible. If we treat it like a stranger, God will be a stranger to us. If we don't know and trust His character, we won't follow Him. We won't rely on Him to rescue us. We won't persevere in tough times.

If we don't believe the Bible, we will fall to false doctrine and beliefs. Satan will place thoughts in our minds—he's a very hard taskmaster. That is why the Bible continually warns about falling into false teaching. What we believe will dictate our behavior.

Suppose you're in church and the fire alarm sounds. If you believe it's a false alarm, you may look around to see what others do but be in no hurry to leave. However, if you begin to see flames in the walls, you'll stampede to the nearest exit. You and I live by what we truly believe.

The Bible acts as a guard against temporary cultural beliefs. I'm sure you can think of something your grandparents believed that embarrasses you today. You may even wonder how they believed it. We must realize that, like us, they were immersed in their culture. They couldn't see beyond what they were taught and what their peers accepted as truth. One day, our grandchildren might be embarrassed over what we believe today. They'll ask themselves, "How could my (smart) grandparents see life in that way?" Tim Keller says we tend to follow the beliefs of the group of people to whom we are drawn. He is not saying that all beliefs are cultural. But left unchecked, we follow the crowd in those beliefs.[11]

Almost everyone has a convincing argument. Otherwise, no one would believe it. People have a tendency to move toward the acceptable. Even when we are "searching" for the truth, we often stumble toward culture. We tend to adapt to the beliefs of those we like, in spite of the evidence. Oftentimes, we only research one side of the issue to justify those beliefs.

The only way to guard against falling into temporary and false cultural beliefs is through knowing Scripture. When we trust God's Word, we stand by it. Our beliefs may cause us persecution or rejection, and others might feel we are backward or ignorant. But in time, the cultural belief will disappear and the truth of God's Word will prevail.

I heard a story about a man called the "human fly." He traveled the country climbing buildings for entertainment purposes. One time, he went to a large city out west. An advertisement declared on a certain day, he would climb up the face of one of the city's large department store buildings. Thousands gathered to watch him perform this seemingly impossible feat. Slowly and carefully, he made his way upward, now clinging to a jutting brick, again to a cornice.

Up and up he went. At last, he was near the top. The crowd watched as he felt to the right and left and then above his head for something firm enough to support his weight. Soon, he seemed to spy what looked like a gray bit of stone or discolored brick protruding from the wall. He reached for it but it was just beyond him. He ventured all and leapt for it and, before the eyes of horrified spectators, he fell to the ground and was broken to pieces. In his hand were the remains of a spider's web! He mistook it for a stone.[12]

What a lesson to stop and think. We must stop grasping for unstable things and anchor ourselves to God, who has our destiny in His hands.

The Bible is also valuable because it leads us to the understanding of God's plan and will for our lives. How can we glorify God? How can we fulfill our lives? We wouldn't know what to do without the Bible.

When we don't trust God's Word, we won't trust how He relates to us in our personal lives. What we see, hear and experience will not connect with our faith. We won't be able to persevere during the tough times.

Sometimes it simply comes down to one question: Do you believe God is sovereign (ruling over all things) or not? Don't you believe that our sovereign God, who loved us enough to send His Son to die for us, would want us to have a perfect communication tool (the Bible), to know Him in a close, personal way?

There are many books in my library. All of them have something in common. They all contain some truth. Some of the books contain more truth than others, but all contain truth. All the books, except one, have a second thing in common. They all contain error. The only book that does not have error is the Bible. I can't go wrong following the teachings and guidance of a book that's always right.

The Bible is God's Word to us. Read it, study it and apply it. My pastor, Bill Ricketts, told a story about dating his wife while in college. He had an opportunity to be a youth camp counselor. The problem was he'd be gone for two weeks and he'd miss his girlfriend, Darla, greatly. A few days into the camp, he received a thick letter from Darla. It was five pages and smelled of her sweet perfume. Though he was excited to get it, he had to go to recreation time with the kids, so he placed it under his pillow.

As the day wore on, he forgot about the letter. Oh, he thought about it occasionally, but it seemed he was always busy when it came to mind. After two weeks at camp, he went home. One of the first things he did was drive to Darla's house. The first thing she asked him was, "Did you read my letter?" Bill replied, "Oh yes, the letter. Wow, it was great to get it, but I really didn't have the time to read it. I had good intentions and I will read it, I promise. But I was just too busy."

How do you think she felt? How do you think God will respond to you when you get to heaven, hand Him your Bible and say, "God I appreciate your letter, but I didn't have time to read it?"

Bill finishes the story, adding, of course, that he didn't treat Darla's letter in this manner. When he received the letter, he opened it immediately and read it over and over again.[13]

God's Word is a key to conquering our spiritual vertigo. What will you do with it?

Discussion Questions

1.   What are some areas where you feel the modern Christian wants to ignore or disbelieve the Bible? Is it regarding money, service, evangelism, moral values?

2. What areas do you struggle with when it comes to believing Scripture?

3. Why is it important to believe all of Scripture? How does this relate to having courageous faith for the future?

Part 3

The Courage We Exercise

7

The Transition

I heard a story about a chemical plant that burned down. Many firefighters tried to put the fire out, but all seemed lost. When the president of the chemical company arrived on the scene, he told the crowd that all their company formulas were in a vault. He offered $100,000 to the team that could put out the fire.

A small volunteer fire team, whose youngest member was over sixty-five years old, sped around the corner. They never slowed down. The driver drove right through the barricades and into the side of the building. The men leapt from the truck and began fighting the fire like no one had ever seen.

Within an hour, the fire was completely out. The president was so elated that he gave the team $200,000. He asked the team's driver, "What are you going to do with all that money?" The driver replied, "Well, the first thing I'm going to do is get the brakes fixed on that truck."

These men were accidental heroes, but God calls us to be intentional heroes. How do we make that happen?

So far, we have said that truth stands between two worlds, the "no longer" and the "not yet." We have looked at the "no longer." We have said that in order to overcome our spiritual vertigo, we must look at the past from God's perspective—with gratitude. We must trust Him and His Word, knowing He is always working in our lives. Seeing what God is doing in us helps us to trust Him. However, what we see is not the whole truth.

Our emphasis has been on dealing with our doubts, but working through our spiritual vertigo must mean more than regaining faith and spiritual balance. Once we are balanced, we need to look forward to the "not yet." We need to do something with our faith. We need to courageously move forward and make an impact in our world.

Knowing that God is always at work in our lives, we can become excited and passionate about what God plans for our future. In John 14:12, Jesus said, "Truly, truly, I say to you, he who believes in Me, the works that I do, he will do also; and greater *works* than these he will do; because I go to the Father."

God wants to do even greater things through us. We are virtually limitless in our potential. Our only limitation is that of God's will for our lives. That is like a minnow complaining that the ocean is too small for him.

How do we turn the corner from the "no longer" to the "not yet"? How do we become lion-chasing, giant-killing machines for Christ? How do we make gratitude for the past lead us to present and future courage? How do we believe God for greater things, even in the midst of struggle? In the Bible, I found no better example of the tension between the battle and the blessing than in the book of Joshua. Here we see the story of the Israelites taking the Promised Land.

In chapter one, Moses died and Joshua succeeded him as Israel's leader. Israel embarked on a physical journey that greatly symbolizes our spiritual journey with Christ. In the next few chapters, I'll take you on a brief trip through this book as we discover truths that will lead us to courageous faith.

As the story begins, the nation of Israel stands poised to enter into the Promised Land. These people had wandered in the wilderness for forty years because of their disobedience at Kadesh-barnea. To give some background, the Israelites had prepared to enter the Promised Land forty years earlier. At that time, Moses sent twelve spies to Canaan to suggest strategies for conquering that land.

Instead of strategies, they returned with recommendations. Ten of the spies came back with negative reports. They said, "We went in to the land where you sent us; and it certainly does flow with milk and honey, and this is its fruit. Nevertheless, the people who live in the land are strong, and the cities are fortified *and* very large; and moreover, we saw the descendants of Anak there" (Num. 13:27–28). The other two spies, Joshua and Caleb, reassured their people: "Then Caleb quieted the people before Moses and said, 'We should by all means go up and take possession of it, for we will surely overcome it'" (13:30).

The Israelite people caught the fear of the first ten spies. Jaded by years of slavery in Egypt, they easily forgot their brief history with God's miracles, including the parting of the Red Sea. They couldn't see past their spiritual vertigo. They took counsel in these fears, rebelled against God, and refused to go into the Promised Land. As a result, God prevented that generation from inheriting Canaan. Instead, they died in the wilderness.

Now, forty years had passed, Moses was dead, and Joshua assumed leadership of Israel. Not only did he need courageous faith, he also had to create an atmosphere of courage amongst his people. How do we begin to look beyond fear and into a hopeful future? How do we join hands with past and future to venture out in faith?

We read in Joshua 1:1–9:

> Now it came about after the death of Moses the servant of the LORD, that the LORD spoke to Joshua the son of Nun, Moses' servant, saying, "Moses My servant is dead; now therefore arise, cross this Jordan, you and all this people, to the land which I am giving to them, to the sons of Israel. Every place on which the sole of your foot treads, I have given it to you, just as I spoke to Moses. From the wilderness and this Lebanon, even as far as the great river, the river Euphrates, all the land of the Hittites, and as far as the Great Sea toward the setting of the sun will be your territory. No man will *be able* to stand before you all the days of your life. Just as I have been with Moses, I will be with you; I will not fail you or forsake you. Be strong and courageous, for you shall give this people possession of the land which I swore to their fathers to give them. Only be strong and very courageous; be careful to do according to all the law which Moses My servant commanded you; do not turn from it to the right or to the left, so that you may have success wherever you go. This book of the law shall not depart from your mouth, but you shall meditate on it day and night, so that you may be careful to do according to all that is written in it; for then you will make your way prosperous, and then you will have success. Have I not commanded you? Be strong and courageous! Do not tremble or be dismayed, for the LORD your God is with you wherever you go."

This passage answers the question "What are the foundational principles of courageous faith?"

The Presence of God

Note God's promise to Joshua. He assured him three times that He would be with him: "Every place on which the sole of your foot treads, I have given it to you, just as I spoke to Moses" (Josh. 1:3). "Just as I have been with Moses, I will be with you" (1:5). "For the LORD your God is with you wherever you go" (1:9).

Joshua had a tough act to follow. For over forty years, Moses led Israel as one of the most influential people in their history. God used him in the performance of many miracles: the ten plagues of Egypt, the parting of the Red Sea, water from a rock and manna (thin pancake wafers) from heaven. When he received the Ten Commandments on Mount Sinai, the people even saw Moses' face shining because he had been in the presence of God.

Deuteronomy 34:10 says, "Since that time no prophet has risen in Israel like Moses, whom the LORD knew face to face." Try to follow that! And now Joshua had to lead them to conquer seven enemy nations. The Israelites proved to be a rebellious, complaining people and they considered Joshua the "number two" guy. It's no wonder God gave him words of comfort in chapter one! God promised five things to Joshua and the Israelite people:

1. Property (Josh. 1:4)
2. Power (1:5)
3. Protection (1:5)
4. Prosperity (1:8)
5. His Presence (1:1, 5, 9)

Their greatest comfort was God's promise to be with Joshua, just as He'd been with Moses. They had no need to fear. How do we have strength to fight? How do we have strength to overcome fears and insecurities? The Bible says, "The joy of the LORD is [our] strength" (Neh. 8:10).

Joy and happiness are not the same thing. Happiness is dependent. When something good happens, we're happier because our circumstances are good. When our circumstances take a negative turn, our happiness does also.

Joy comes from the inside. It's peace, hope and satisfaction in God, despite outward circumstances. We experience joy when we have peace in the midst of turmoil. We experience hope as we step into the unknown. We find satisfaction and pleasure in Christ, not in the things He has created. Through this joyful presence, we find spiritual balance.

This joy gives us strength to overcome discouragement. It brings committed passion for Christ and the future He holds. It brings courageous faith into our hearts as we learn to place greater trust in Him. How do we receive this joy? Psalm 16:11 tells us it comes from God's presence in our lives: "You will make known to me the path of life; / In Your presence is fullness of joy; / In Your right hand there are pleasures forever." The key to strength is joy; the avenue to joy is God's presence.

Of course, this begs an important question: What do I mean by God's presence? Doesn't the Holy Spirit (God's presence) come into our hearts the moment we become Christians? Yes! Isn't God's presence everywhere in the world? Yes! But the Bible teaches God's presence on three levels:

1. He is omnipresent. That doesn't mean that we all feel His presence all the time.

2. He indwells the Christian. "But if the Spirit of Him who raised Jesus from the dead dwells in you, He who raised Christ Jesus from the dead will also give life to your mortal bodies through His Spirit who dwells in you" (Rom. 8:11). That doesn't mean every Christian consistently feels His presence in their lives.

3. The Bible describes His manifest presence as the times we sense Him in our lives. These are the times when He reveals His glory to us.

One pastor spoke of God's presence in his son's life. He asked, "Son, when did you first truly feel God's presence in your life?" His son recalled that it was when he was a young boy. At that time, his dad met with other men to pray in the "upper room" of their church before the Sunday evening service. The pastor's son, looking for his dad, realized he was in prayer with the men. The boy walked in and knelt down beside his dad. As the men prayed aloud together, he felt the powerful presence of God in the room. It was his first encounter with God's manifest presence.

To Joshua, God's presence meant an act that would affirm his leadership, just as He'd done with Moses. It meant God would give him wisdom and direction. It meant God would do whatever was necessary to bring about His promise to Israel. God commanded Joshua to be strong, courageous and fearless. If Joshua obeyed, God would do the rest.

Much of our fear comes from insecurity and the unknown. We fear for our jobs, failure, change, people, embarrassment, and even our physical well-being. What would happen if we felt God's manifest presence in our life right now? How would that give us the security we need?

A good description of security is the feeling that a responsible person cares about you. God is that responsible person. When we sense His presence, there is a newfound courage. It's better than flashing a detective's badge, knowing the entire police force and government are behind us. It's more powerful than the authority to make major decisions, knowing our company stands behind us.

Security comes from the knowledge that the most loving, responsible, powerful and gracious Being in the universe is with us and cares for us. It empowers courage that's willing to venture, reach out and risk for the cause of Christ. Do you sense His presence in your life? Let me encourage you to find time daily to be alone with God. Read the Bible. Pray for God's presence to fill your heart.

A Clear Purpose

To have courageous faith, we must not only realize God's presence but have a clear purpose as well. We need a cause that's worth the risk. In any venture, we must ask, "What are we doing? What's the purpose or the goal?" Earlier I said we need clarity in a situation to feel compelled to action. As Andy Stanley says, we love ambiguity because as soon as a situation becomes clear, we're compelled to act.[1]

Stanley's example is the story of the good Samaritan, which begins with a lawyer who tried to entrap Jesus. He asked, "Teacher, what shall I do to inherit eternal life?" Jesus said to him, "What is written in the Law? How does it read to you?" The lawyer answered, "You shall love the Lord your God with all your heart, and with all your soul, and with all your strength, and with all your mind; and your neighbor as yourself." Jesus replied, "You have answered correctly; Do this and you will live." The lawyer then asked, "Who is my neighbor?" (see Luke 10:25-37).

The shrewd lawyer tried to brush off any responsibility by making the term "neighbor" ambiguous. To many, a neighbor could be anyone. To some Jews, it meant only the Jewish people.[2] Instead of allowing truth to embrace his heart, the lawyer wanted to muddy the discussion by turning a question back to Jesus. But the parable of the good Samaritan clarified that our neighbor is anyone in need.

Sometimes we feel more comfortable living in a fog. We claim we want to know God's will; but in some ways, we're more comfortable with not knowing. We take comfort in our ignorance, hoping that it might somehow exempt us from the responsibility of following God's Word.

Clarity can lead to faith and faith to passion. Not long after my call to ministry, I remember sitting back in a comfortable chair, minding my own business, when God hit me with a question: "What is My will for your life?" I then asked myself what my ministry would encompass. After a brief time in prayer, God made it clear that, based on my gifts and ministry burden, He desired two things:

1. Evangelism: reach as many people for Christ as possible in my lifetime.
2. Spiritual growth: teach as many people as God would allow in my lifetime.

My life verses are found in First Corinthians 2:4–5, which reads, "My message and my preaching were not in persuasive words of wisdom, but in demonstration of the Spirit and of power, so that your faith would not rest on the wisdom of men, but on the power of God." The purpose and priority of the decisions I've made as a pastor always centered on those two things. My leadership may not have always been popular with everyone. However, no one ever needed to question my motives behind the decisions.

Joshua had a clear vision—a mandate and purpose from God. In Joshua 1:3–4, we read, "Every place on which the sole of your foot treads, I have given it to you, just as I spoke to Moses. From the wilderness and this Lebanon, even as far as the great river, the river Euphrates, all the land of the Hittites, and as far as the Great Sea toward the setting of the sun will be your territory." The Israelites soon crossed the Jordan River border of Canaan. God gave Joshua the boundaries of their inheritance: from the wilderness (the area of desert south and east) to the far northeast borders at the Euphrates River to the land of the Hittites (modern-day Syria) and the western boundary at the Mediterranean Sea.

Backing up to Joshua 1:2, God says, "I am giving." Then in 1:3, He says, "I have given." Which is it? It is both! God gave it to them. That is faith vision. I am giving—that is the action. God says I already gave it to you as far as the promises are concerned. The deed to the land is yours. But if you want it, you'll have to take it. Joshua's purpose, what he'd been born for, was to courageously lead the Israelites into the Promised Land and claim God's promises.

A Compelling Vision

The Bible says, "Where there is no vision, the people are unrestrained, / But happy is he who keeps the law" (Prov. 29:18).

Without vision, there's no true clarity or direction. How do we define vision? Jazz musician Duke Ellington once said, "If you got rhythm, you don't need no definition. And if you don't have it, ain't no definition gonna help."[3]

It's difficult to define vision, especially in light of the heavenly visions found in the Bible. When I speak of vision, I'm not referring to the supernatural, physical manifestations from heaven. Spiritual vision is motivation from God, giving us direction through glimpses of a future that could be.

Joshua had a life purpose. God motivated Joshua through a vision for his future. As stated previously, Joshua 1:4 is like a geographical map. Not only do we need motivation, we need direction. Vision can be a guiding force to our destination. A few years ago, my mother suffered a stroke. My family assured me she would be fine, but I still felt the need to check on her. The problem was, I live near Orlando and my parents lived near Athens, Georgia, which was about a nine-hour drive from my home. One of the men in our church, Rocky, had previously told me that he owned a plane and if I ever needed to travel anywhere, he would take me. I called him and we decided that he would fly me to Athens and back on the same day.

During the flight, he asked if I'd like to fly the plane. I answered, "Yes!" After some instrument panel flight instruction, I took the yoke. I tried to fly by the little needle in front of my face, but found it difficult to fly straight. I'd veer off the line each time and overcorrect. After veering back and forth for fifteen minutes, Rocky thought he'd better take over again since we needed to get there before dark.

On the way back, Rocky asked me if I wanted to try again. Anxious to make up for my less-than-stellar beginning, I said yes. This time, he told me to pick a point in the clouds or the landscape below and fly towards it, occasionally checking the instruments. I found that when I looked ahead instead of right in front of me, it gave me perspective. I guided the plane rather than constantly overcorrecting.

Sometimes in life, we only see what's right in front of us. We have nearsighted spiritual vision. We tend to react and overcorrect when faced with adverse circumstances. But when we look out on the horizon, envisioning God's future for us rather than panicking, we simply make the necessary minor adjustments.

Vision not only gives us hope and direction, it points to future faith. Connecting the dots of faith vision is the "not yet" of belief. Hebrews 11:1 says, "Now faith is the assurance of *things* hoped for, the conviction of things not seen." Faith is not all vision—it's also the conviction of things not seen.

However, the assurance of things hoped for speaks of a visionary life, a hope for the future. For example, I don't know what heaven is like. I've never been there, but I hear it's nice. In fact, a good preacher can take Revelation's final chapters and help listeners envision a beautiful picture of it. A vision like that will make you want to pack your bags and go today! This is our afterlife vision. It is our hope. It's our guiding light to the future.

The heroes of faith in Hebrews 11 had vision.

> All these died in faith, without receiving the promises, but having seen them and having welcomed them from a distance, and having confessed that they were strangers and exiles on the earth. For those who say such things make it clear that they are seeking a country of their own. And indeed if they had been thinking of that

> *country* from which they went out, they would have had
> opportunity to return. But as it is, they desire a better
> *country*, that is, a heavenly one. Therefore God is not
> ashamed to be called their God; for He has prepared a
> city for them. (11:13-16)

These heroes looked to a better country—heaven. The vision was worth the inconvenience, the work and the suffering they often encountered.

While purpose is a lifetime call, vision can be for a specific period. I mentioned my two life purposes. For me, the purposes for preaching and evangelism haven't changed but my vision for accomplishing these purposes has.

When I graduated from seminary, Pam and I moved to Atlanta, where we planted a church. We had a vision to build a strong, viable church and in just three years, that vision came to fulfillment. We had a twenty thousand square foot building, five acres of land, and averaged 130 attendees. During the next five years, we grew to 325 in attendance, constituted ourselves as a church, and started two mission churches.

I remember asking God, "Now what? What's the next vision?" After considerable prayer, I felt God speak to my heart that one day I would pastor a church with over two thousand in attendance, complete with missions and new ministries. Although that sounds like an ego feed, I had no desire to pastor a church that large at that time.

When I announced this vision to my church, there was little excitement. It's not that they disbelieved we could do it. They just weren't sure they wanted it. I believed we would accomplish this vision at our Atlanta church. After all, I planned to stay at that church for the rest of my life. But God had other plans.

Life changed one snowy Sunday morning in Georgia (yes, it snows occasionally). It was the worst storm I had ever experienced. There were eight inches of snow on the ground and every church in the city called off services. That afternoon, I walked in from the store to find my wife on the phone with a man from Florida. She handed me the phone and whispered, "It's a man from a pastor search committee in Florida." Three months later, I became their pastor.

As far as our hearts were concerned, this change didn't happen overnight. We had wrestled for months prior concerning God's future for us. The struggle was painful because we truly loved the people at our church and loved being near our families in Georgia. For me, the struggle continued well after moving to Florida. Why did God give me this vision for the future of my church and then move me? Although purposes are permanent, visions only last a season. God brought His vision for my life to fruition, just in another location. He gave me a glimpse for direction. As I moved closer to reality, the vision became clearer.

Do you have a life purpose? Do you see God's vision for you? Once our purpose and vision are clear, we begin to have clarity. That moves us to action.

An Obedience to God's Vision

"Then Joshua commanded the officers of the people, saying, 'Pass through the midst of the camp and command the people, saying, "Prepare provisions for yourselves, for within three days you are to cross this Jordan, to go in to possess the land which the LORD your God is giving you, to possess it"'" (Josh. 1:10-11).

Joshua tells the people to prepare themselves. They had three days to get ready to take the land the Lord gave them. They first needed clarity and to ask themselves, "What do we need to do?" Then, they needed action.

Obedience is a foundational truth for courageous faith. You may ask, "What if I don't succeed? What if the giant wins or the lion eats me? What if I get embarrassed and make a fool of myself?"

I wish I could tell you that there are no risks involved. No courage would be necessary if we didn't have some fear and uncertainty. I can't promise that every single action will meet with success and personal glory. I can't say you'll never receive criticism or embarrassment. But the story in Joshua encourages me! Every time the Israelites obeyed God, He blessed them. Every time they either disobeyed or failed to consult God, they suffered a setback.

I can also encourage you that, while not every action you take will result in success, everything will work together for your good. The promise of Romans 8:28 is "And we know that God causes all things to work together for good to those who love God, to those who are called according to *His* purpose." "All things together" means that in the end, all things work out for your good. I've heard it said that if it's not good, then it's not the end.

God created us for action. When He gives us strength, vision and direction, it's time to pursue diligently. The Israelites knew that nothing worthwhile comes cheap. There's always a price to pay—either up front with later benefit, or with ease today and a heavy price later, maybe in a wasted life. It all depends on what we want most out of life.

I'm like you. I want to succeed. I'm tempted to take the counsel of my ego and my fears. Sometimes, I wonder why God should make me a giant-slayer instead of the next person. In times like these, I ask myself these questions: "Who am I trying to glorify? Am I first in my life or is God? Am I trying to use God to make me a hero or do I want to be used to make Christ the hero?" If my motives are right, I know God will bless me and make all things work for good in the end, and for His glory.

God's presence, purpose and vision, coupled with our obedience to follow Him, are all vital to keep our spiritual balance and to move forward with courageous faith.

Discussion Questions

1. Have you ever felt God's manifest presence in your life? Can you describe it?
2. How would your life be different if you could experience His manifest presence in your life on a consistent basis? Be specific. How would it affect your family, job, disposition, etc.?
3. What is your purpose in life? Why are you here?
4. What action have you been putting off? What have you not acted on that God has led you to do?

8

Going for It

Life can be defined by the opportunities we seize.

As a young man, I received many opportunities to preach at youth meetings and general revivals in many small churches. One pastor would tell another about me, which led to multiple new opportunities. That's how I started in the ministry.

One such pastor, David, pastored a small country church. He had been bivocational for many years and longed to be able to pastor on a full-time basis. He invited me to preach a week of meetings. The services went well—many came to know Christ. We became good friends. In one of our conversations, he told me that a church was interviewing him for a full-time pastorate. I had never seen him more excited. He loved his present church, but the opportunity to give up his full-time job and devote all of his time to the ministry would be his dream come true.

Not long after our conversation, that church asked him to be their pastor. David accepted the call. When he announced to his present church that he was leaving, the congregation had a great outpouring of emotion. People begged him to stay. Leaders called him on the phone, crying and pleading for him to reconsider. Moved by his love for them, my friend told the new church he had reconsidered. While this may seem very loyal to you, David soon realized he might have missed God's will. His personality seemed to change. He became somewhat cynical and apathetic toward ministry. He seemed tired and lost hope of any relief.

A few years later, there was a disagreement over some designated money given to the church. David wanted to do what was right and legal, but the leaders wanted to spend the money for something different. The disagreement ended in David's termination. The church that had loved him and begged him to stay eventually fired him. David found another church, but he was never able to work in a ministry full-time. Today, I think he'd say he missed an opportunity.

As I said earlier, the number one regret of successful people isn't something they did, but opportunities they missed. It's been said that life can be defined by the decisions we make. Think about this in terms of time and combine all the time it takes to make decisions.

When we add up the sum of the time it took to make decisions about school, jobs, marriage and other milestones, our life can be summed up in just a few hours. All of us want to grab opportunity by the mane. We want to excel, accelerate and make a difference, but fear and doubt envelop us. Life's "what ifs" ricochet through our mind.

What if I fail? What if I don't have enough money? What if others fail me? What if I get hurt? We fear the dark, the unknown and the new. These fears affect our decisions, which often cause us to miss our opportunities.

Faith's reach stands between the "no longer" and the "not yet." Let's spring forward to the "not yet." How can we use the past, our gratitude and our present experiences with God to propel us into the future? How can we keep ourselves from falling back into spiritual vertigo?

Looking at chapter one of Joshua, God gave the Israelites a great promise. Verses 8–9 say, "This book of the law shall not depart from your mouth, but you shall meditate on it day and night, so that you may be careful to do according to all that is written in it; for then you will make your way prosperous, and then you will have success. Have I not commanded you? Be strong and courageous! Do not tremble or be dismayed, for the LORD your God is with you wherever you go." Now God begins to lead the Israelites toward their future—their opportunity. For years, they heard their elders tell of milk and honey in the Promised Land. They dreamed about it. Now, it was about to happen.

How do we seize opportunities? How do we propel into the future with assurance?

God Has Gone Ahead of You

> Then Joshua rose early in the morning; and he and all the sons of Israel set out from Shittim and came to the Jordan, and they lodged there before they crossed. At the end of three days the officers went through the midst of the camp; and they commanded the people, saying, "When you see the ark of the covenant of the LORD your God with the Levitical priests carrying it, then you shall set out from your place and go after it. However, there shall be between you and it a distance of about 2,000 cubits by measure. Do not come near it, that you may know the way by which you shall go, for you have not passed this way before." (Josh. 3:1–4)

It's one thing to know God's presence in our life. It's another to realize He goes before us in the journey.

The ark of the covenant was a wooden box with a golden lid. It contained God's law transcribed by Moses. Beside it was the mercy seat. The high priest of Israel would sprinkle the blood of a goat on this seat to atone for the sins of Israel in the coming year. The most significant aspect of the ark is that it represented God's presence in Israel. So awesome was the ark, that when placed in the Holy of Holies inside the Tabernacle, a veil or curtain separated it.

No one could go behind the veil except the high priest and then only once annually. If the priest touched the ark, even mistakenly, God would strike him down and he would die. In his Gospel, Matthew gave an account that upon Jesus' death on the cross, the hand of God tore the veil in half. This signified the end of separation from God—that once and for all, Christ atoned for our sins and gave us full access to God.

Looking back at Joshua 3, we see a vivid example of man's separation from God. The Lord gave Joshua instructions to take the ark with them . . . at a distance. The two thousand cubits (one thousand yards) were close enough to see, be inspired by, and be guided by the ark, but far enough away to demonstrate the needed separation from a holy God. When we venture into our promised land, God will go before us: "You go before me and follow me. / You place your hand of blessing on my head" (Ps. 139:5, NLT).

While in college, my church group attended a large conference in Atlanta, fifty miles away from the school. Each day that week, we loaded forty people on a bus and made the trip. The conference went until ten o'clock each evening, so getting back home made for a long night. One evening, after a particularly great session, God flooded my heart. He lifted my burdens and I was on fire for Him.

When we returned to our bus, it wouldn't start. The youth pastor sent three of our youth over to the bus depot to call for help (there were no cell phones back then). When I heard what he'd done, I could hardly believe it! The bus depot was one of the most dangerous places in downtown Atlanta. I immediately went after them.

I suppose you need some background. I had the opportunity to intern at one of the churches in downtown Atlanta the year prior to this particular trip. Growing up in nearby Athens, I knew the dangers of Atlanta. As an intern, I never walked alone downtown at night. Even in the daytime, in an area filled with drug dealers and strip clubs, I walked carefully and never looked anyone in the eye.

Fast forward a year later and here I was boldly walking to the most dangerous place in the murder capital of America. On my way, a man wearing a black coat and a white hat stopped me. He offered me any woman or drug I desired—for a price. Surrounded by dozens of his friends, I shared the gospel with him. I looked around and discovered his friends were walking toward us, not to confront me, but to listen. Just then, the three youth members spotted me as they came out of the bus station. With the interruption, the moment was broken, but I believe that somehow God used that witness.

What made the difference for me? Why wasn't I afraid? Because I felt God going before me. That evening, I sensed the presence and power of God in my life. In that moment, God's presence in my life was more important than the clear and present danger. My newfound compassion for the drug dealer had higher priority than my physical well-being. I probably would have been afraid the night before, but not that night.

God's presence also teaches us His character. To know someone, we must be close to them. The ark represented God's presence, which let the Israelites see God through His actions in their lives. They witnessed the parting of the Jordan River. They witnessed food falling from heaven to feed them in the wilderness. The Israelites witnessed God's provision—even their sandals lasted forty years! They experienced Gods love, promises, grace and mercy. They also felt His wrath and judgment, and witnessed His power and sovereignty.

As a believer, I come to know God through His Word, but I also witness His works in my life when He draws close. When I sense God's presence, I become bolder.

We Must Prepare Ourselves

Henry Ford once said, "Before everything else, getting ready is the secret of success."[1] Famed British conservative writer and prime minister Benjamin Disraeli said, "One secret of success in life is for a man to be ready for his opportunity when it comes."[2]

In order to propel ourselves courageously into the future, we must be prepared. Anything worthwhile requires preparation. Soldiers go through boot camp, ballplayers shape up in spring training, and college students take classes to prepare for life. In verses 3–5 of Joshua 3, Joshua challenges God's people, "Consecrate yourselves, for tomorrow the LORD will do wonders among you."

Here, to consecrate oneself means "to sanctify or make holy." Individuals were instructed to cleanse the sin from their lives in preparation. As we prepare for the future, we must first deal with our past.

In anticipation of God's great wonders, let me suggest a few ways to prepare.

Deal with the Past

One way we deal with our past is to confess and repent for our sins. It's true Christ saved us by grace, but a cleansed walk with God helps us appreciate what He gave us at salvation. First John 1:9 tells every Christian we must still confess our sins: "If we confess our sins, He is faithful and righteous to forgive us our sins and to cleanse us from all unrighteousness."

Sin separates us from fellowship with God, gradually destroying our concept of Him. I remember a young man who told me he would live his own way until he was thirty. Once married, then he would receive Christ. This is, of course, problematic on so many fronts.

When we aren't walking with God, we risk making bad life decisions. If we expect God's guidance, we can't predetermine God's grace. We must be upright so God can speak to us, go before us, and do great things through us. I explained to the young man that when we fail to confess our sins to the Lord, it distorts our view of God. Sin destroys the moral fiber of our soul. We lose the concept of God's love, grace and holiness, thereafter leaving our faith damaged.

We not only need to confess our past but also move on from it. Often our movement toward the future lacks force and freedom because we carry baggage from our past. For example, one of the greatest marital problems is the baggage brought by each individual into the relationship. Unresolved conflicts with parents, past sins and unrealistic expectations are just a few examples of emotional luggage that can challenge a couple's marriage.

Until we deal with this baggage, the marital relationship will suffer. The guilt from past sins and bad habits will handicap us as we move toward the future. Baggage is always a heavy burden. It's like arriving at the airport only to realize the airline charges an additional twenty dollars for carry-on bags and forty dollars for checked luggage. Extra baggage carries a price and often takes us by surprise.

Face Your Fears

As we move forward to the future, we again consider our "what ifs." What are you afraid of? Failure? Loss? Embarrassment? Rejection? All of us have fears. I face my own in three ways:

1. I imagine the worst outcome and face it. It's usually not as bad as I thought.
2. I make Christ my priority. No one can take the most precious thing in my life away. I must value my relationship with Jesus far more than any task or blessing. He *is* my greatest blessing.
3. I remind myself that accomplishing hard and fearful things is good for me. It builds character and faith.

The late President John F. Kennedy said, "We ... do [these] things not because they are easy, but because they are hard."[3] Doing the hard things moves us along in our journey from doubt to courageous faith.

We Must Take the Step of Faith

Even with the knowledge that God went before us, preparing ourselves to follow takes faith, but it's not complete faith. Eventually, courageous faith must act.

In Joshua 3:6–13, Joshua shares with the people how God will accomplish crossing the Jordan.

> And Joshua spoke to the priests, saying, "Take up the ark of the covenant and cross over ahead of the people." So they took up the ark of the covenant and went ahead of the people.
>
> Now the LORD said to Joshua, "This day I will begin to exalt you in the sight of all Israel, that they may know that just as I have been with Moses, I will be with you. You shall, moreover, command the priests who are carrying the ark of the covenant, saying, 'When you come to the edge of the waters of the Jordan, you shall stand *still* in the Jordan.'" Then Joshua said to the sons of Israel, "Come here, and hear the words of the LORD your God." Joshua said, "By this you shall know that the living God is among you, and that He will assuredly dispossess from before you the Canaanite, the Hittite, the Hivite, the Perizzite, the Girgashite, the Amorite, and the Jebusite. Behold, the ark of the covenant of the Lord of all the earth is crossing over ahead of you into the Jordan. Now then, take for yourselves twelve men from the tribes of Israel, one man for each tribe. It shall come about when the soles of the feet of the priests who carry the ark of the LORD, the Lord of all the earth, rest in the waters of the Jordan, the waters of the Jordan will be cut off, *and* the waters which are flowing down from above will stand in one heap."

Verses 14–17 of Joshua 3 summarize how it happened.

> So when the people set out from their tents to cross the Jordan with the priests carrying the ark of the covenant before the people, and when those who carried the ark came into the Jordan, and the feet of the priests carrying the ark were dipped in the edge of the water (for the Jordan overflows all its banks all the days of harvest), the waters which were flowing down from above stood *and* rose up in one heap, a great distance away at Adam, the city that is beside Zarethan; and those which were flowing down toward the sea of the Arabah, the Salt Sea, were completely cut off. So the people crossed opposite Jericho. And the priests who carried the ark of the covenant of the LORD stood firm on dry ground in the middle of the Jordan while all Israel crossed on dry ground, until all the nation had finished crossing the Jordan.

When I was in Israel a few years ago, I visited the Jordan River. The water isn't extremely deep but the riverbanks drop off suddenly. There is no gradual step, like going from the beach into the ocean. So while everyone else took a small step of faith, the priests who cared for the ark took a much larger one.

The ark was supported by two poles on either of the elongated sides. It took four priests to lift up and carry the ark by these two poles.

If the priests touched the ark, they would immediately die. The sudden drop, coupled with muddy water, made it impossible to see where their feet would land. If the water didn't part and place them on dry land when the priests stepped into it, they'd fall into the river. The ark would fall and most certainly come in contact with them.

This parting of the Jordan River served Israel in three ways:

1. It authenticated Joshua's leadership, emulating the miracle God did for Moses when He parted the Red Sea. It's important for followers to know that their leader has God's hand upon them.
2. It built the people's faith. They heard about Moses and the parting of the Red Sea from their leaders. Now they see God's hand is upon them, as well.
3. It melted the heart of the enemy. When we accomplish God's will and move forward with zeal, we melt the heart of our enemy!

Every new venture, every new decision, every confrontation with fear, requires a step of faith in the midst of struggle. Sometimes the future seems dark and murky. We can't see where our foot will land. But if it were easy, everyone would do it.

Coming to Christ for salvation is our first step of faith into the unknown. The one facing this decision might ask: How is my life going to change? What will people think of me? Will I lose my friends? What will this church expect of me? What do I have to give up? A person may weigh their choices first; but as the Spirit draws them, they'll take the step of faith and go for it, realizing that nothing else compares to knowing Christ.

As believers, our decision to follow Christ in specific areas of our lives also requires a step into the unknown. We see this in the area of giving. Can I afford to give? What will I have to give up? Will God provide?

We also see the challenge in the area of forgiving others. Will they really pay for what they did? Should I want them to pay? Will there be another confrontation? Will they apologize?

Whatever the decision, we must take a step of faith to experience God's "not yet." Security may be on the shore, but the miracle is in the river. Where does God want you to step out in faith right now?

Follow Through

Sometimes the most important decision is the one we make right after the original decision—for example, feeling convicted in a worship service to begin reading our Bible every day. That is an important decision.

However, the more important decision is the one we make when we get out of bed the next morning. Are we going to get up early enough to read the Bible? Joshua 3:17 reads, "And the priests who carried the ark of the covenant of the LORD stood firm on dry ground in the middle of the Jordan while all Israel crossed on dry ground, until all the nation had finished crossing the Jordan." The Israelites crossed the Jordan, but they never finished taking the Promised Land. The problems they faced were similar to those we face today. Life was challenging. Once they conquered a particular area of land, they farmed it to provide for their families. These everyday life tasks often derail us from following through. I'll address this more completely in chapter 13; but for now, it's important that I share a few insights with you.

The Israelites faced some tough opposition. Many of the Canaanite leaders fought against them. People lied to them and formed ungodly alliances. It's tough to keep moving forward when we're always celebrating victories or feeling battle fatigue. We often come up short, believing "I've done enough." I call this "the level of satisfaction" or the "survival line."

I witnessed this "survival line" myself. As I mentioned, after seminary, Pam and I moved back to Georgia to plant a church. We recruited about thirty people from the sponsoring church and quickly added more from the community. We began at a day care center. After outgrowing that facility, we moved to a nearby school. In the beginning days, everyone worked hard. We had few "consumers" or "customers," as our people saw what was at stake. They had a wartime mind-set. Everyone pulled together for the greater cause. They felt a sense of ownership.

After two and a half years, we moved into a new building and grew to the point where we could pay all the bills. At that point, something began to change. Some of our people no longer had a passion for the work. They loved the church but became "satisfied." Subconsciously, they felt they had gone far enough. They found satisfaction at the "survival line."

When we were a mission church, the threat and fear of not making it was real. We knew we must work hard, pray hard and come together to be successful. However, the definition of success, for some, was survival. Once we moved into a building, fully constituted and viable, these well-meaning, God-loving people began to rest. But God's plans are always greater than survival.

I witnessed the same satisfaction among pastors and staff. When I was in seminary, a very well-known church set many baptism and attendance records. I happened to be working with their staff on a project when the pastor announced they were taking a year off from new ministries.

This church was at the forefront of innovation, evangelism and church growth. Fatigue had set in and the pastor felt it would be healthier to manage current tasks and projects. This might not seem like a bad idea, but this church never regained momentum. The pastor spent the last years of his ministry at a standstill. As one friend put it, "The pastor put the church on hold for fifteen years."

I challenge you to follow God's path *completely*. God wants much more for you than you ever thought possible. "'I know the plans that I have for you,' declares the LORD, 'plans for welfare and not for calamity to give you a future and a hope'" (Jer. 29:11). God wants us to keep our passionate mind-set far beyond the survival line. He wants us to continue to work, going forward to claim all the blessings He promised.

I heard a story about a mountain-climbing expedition for tourists where a guide took climbers up a tall mountain. In the middle of the trip, they stopped midway up the mountain at a resort-style cabin. This place served flavored coffees and food. It had a warm and inviting atmosphere with a large fireplace and a grand piano in the middle of a rustic-style room.

The proprietor of the shop often noticed how climbers responded to the warmth of the cabin. All the climbers came in cold and tired. The guide allowed the climbers about twenty minutes to drink their coffee and take a rest, then reassembled the group to finish the climb. In nearly every expedition, the proprietor said some of the climbers decided to stay behind. They felt they had a good climbing experience and wanted to relax and have fun.

Those left behind initially had a good time—playing the piano, laughing and talking. But as time went by and they anticipated their friends would reach the top of the mountain, they quieted. Sadness permeated each group as they realized the excitement their friends were experiencing. They'd sacrificed the opportunity to have the same elation for a moment of rest and leisure.

Opportunities will come your way. Don't hesitate when they do. Take the step of faith to seize them. Go for it!

Discussion Questions

1. What opportunity do you feel you missed? Why do you think you missed it?
2. What fear is keeping you from your present opportunity?
3. Have you stopped short of your dream? Have you become satisfied with survival instead of pursuing success?
4. What is your next step to get ready to seize your opportunity?

9

Beating the Odds

Sometimes we feel the odds are stacked against us. The popular movie *Braveheart* tells the story of William Wallace, who led the Scottish rebellion against England near the end of the thirteenth century.

In the now-infamous scene, "The Battle of Stirling Bridge," the Scots prepare to go into battle against the English. In response to one soldier's fear and pleas for retreat, Wallace says,

> "I *am* William Wallace, and I see a whole army of my countrymen here in defiance of tyranny! You have come to fight as free men, and free men you are! What will you do without freedom?"
>
> Two thousand against ten?" the veteran shouted. "No, we will run and live!"
>
> "Yes!" Wallace shouted back, "Fight and you may die. Run and you will live, at least awhile. And dying in your bed, many years from now, would you be willing to trade all the days, from this day to that, for one chance, just *one* chance, to come back here as young men and tell our enemies that they may take our lives, but they will *never* take our freedom!"[1]

The Scots won the battle. That battle, and the legend of William Wallace, inspired Scotland to achieve their goal of independence. Each time I hear that speech, it creates passion in me.

Sometimes we want to move forward with God but we feel the odds are stacked against us. It seems like there are walls we can't penetrate, people we can't influence and problems we can't solve. It is during such times that spiritual vertigo can overtake us. We don't want to fail. We don't want to lose. But how do we know if the obstacles before us are tests or stop signs from God? As we continue our journey through the book of Joshua, we find in chapter 6 that the Israelites are about to conquer the first city, Jericho. This scriptural passage lays the guidelines for taking new territory in the midst of great opposition. This chapter will explain those guidelines in plain language.

Discern the Will of God

Finding God's will should be easy. Unfortunately, I have found that is not always the case. In Joshua 6:1–5, we find the need to hear from God.

> Now Jericho was tightly shut because of the sons of Israel; no one went out and no one came in. The LORD said to Joshua, "See, I have given Jericho into your hand, with its king *and* the valiant warriors. You shall march around the city, all the men of war circling the city once. You shall do so for six days. Also seven priests shall carry seven trumpets of rams' horns before the ark; then on the seventh day you shall march around the city seven times, and the priests shall blow the trumpets. It shall be that when they make a long blast with the ram's horn, and when you hear the sound of the trumpet, all

the people shall shout with a great shout; and the wall of the city will fall down flat, and the people will go up every man straight ahead."

Jericho is one of the oldest cities in recorded civilization. We can find it on the east side of the promised land of Canaan. When we look at a map, it's surprising to find Jericho on the border opposite the one with Egypt.[2]

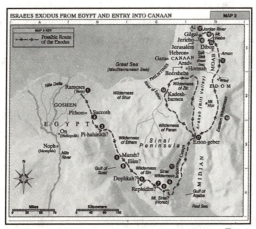

Fig. 4.

It's curious that God led the Israelites through the eastern (rather than the western) border of Canaan, making the trip much longer for the people.

First, He led them south around the Red Sea, and then north, up the east side of Canaan where we find Jericho. The Bible tells us that the shorter route would see much opposition and cause discouragement. This tells us that God is aware of our feelings and fears. He knows how far to push us as we go through trials. He won't give us more than we can bear.

Notice in verse one, the city is tightly shut. This illustrates a seemingly impossible situation, but God had a plan. He gave them steps just for taking Jericho—not the entire land. God spoke first to their leader, Joshua, who then spoke to the people.

> So Joshua the son of Nun called the priests and said to them, "Take up the ark of the covenant, and let seven priests carry seven trumpets of rams' horns before the ark of the Lord." Then he said to the people, "Go forward, and march around the city, and let the armed men go on before the ark of the Lord." And it was *so*, that when Joshua had spoken to the people, the seven priests carrying the seven trumpets of rams' horns before the Lord went forward and blew the trumpets; and the ark of the covenant of the Lord followed them. The armed men went before the priests who blew the trumpets, and the rear guard came after the ark, while they continued to blow the trumpets. But Joshua commanded the people, saying, "You shall not shout nor let your voice be heard nor let a word proceed out of your mouth, until the day I tell you, 'Shout!' Then you shall shout!" So he had the ark of the Lord taken around the city, circling *it* once; then they came into the camp and spent the night in the camp. (Josh. 6:6–11)

God led the battle. It was His fight.

Once you move forward, the vital question becomes, "What does God want me to do?" Answer that and the only other question is, "Am I willing to do it?" There are four prominent ways God communicates His will. All four involve the Scripture and prayer:

1. The commands of God's Word
2. The principles of God's Word
3. The wisdom of God's Word
4. The peace of God's Word

When we look at a passage, we must ask ourselves, "Is there a command for me to obey?" Some things in Scripture are very clear. For example, we know murder, adultery, lying and stealing are wrong. God spelled that out in the Ten Commandments.

When there's no direct command, we turn to the principles of God's Word. There's a great example in First Corinthians 8, where Paul wrote concerning eating meat offered to idols. We may think that's a large section of Scripture on a subject that has nothing to do with us.

Yet, there's a principle there. The passage explains that some Christians had no issues eating meat formerly used in sacrifice to an idol. Others felt it was a sin. Paul simply argued that the meat was fine for consumption since the idols were not gods, that there is only one God and these little statues were not Him.

However, if eating the meat caused another believer to have a guilty conscience, those who ate became stumbling blocks to their Christian brother. The principle is: although a certain activity might not be sin, if it causes our brother to sin or hurts his conscience, then we must refrain from the activity because our brothers and sisters in Christ are more important than our freedom in Christ. Mark 12:30–31 teaches, "'YOU SHALL LOVE THE LORD YOUR GOD WITH ALL YOUR HEART, AND WITH ALL YOUR SOUL, AND WITH ALL YOUR MIND, AND WITH ALL YOUR STRENGTH.' The second is this, 'YOU SHALL LOVE YOUR NEIGHBOR AS YOURSELF.' There is no other commandment greater than these." God comes first, then others, then you.

Each day, we face situations where neither a command nor a principle applies. What then? We must rely on God's wisdom. James 1:5 says, "But if any of you lacks wisdom, let him ask of God, who gives to all generously and without reproach, and it will be given to him." We attain God's wisdom by consistent Bible reading. Saturating the mind with Scripture leads us to the mind of Christ (1 Cor. 2:16) for discerning God's will. There are abundant situations that no biblical chapter or verse addresses. One of my professors once told me he would not move forward on any decision unless a specific verse from the Lord spoke to him.

Unfortunately, there's no verse, in its true interpretation, that will tell us where to attend college or which job to accept. In fact, this approach often leads to taking verses out of context and applying them in ways God never intended.

So what do we do? We rely on God's wisdom given through the work of the Holy Spirit. Andy Stanley wrote a book entitled *The Best Question Ever*. In it, he poses the best question: "What is the wise thing for me to do?"[3] But even this question becomes difficult if we tend toward rationalization to do what we want instead.

That's why it's important to have people around us who possess godly wisdom, who are willing to be honest with us. Although hearing from God is fundamental to our Christian walk, we must realize we often need others' perspectives too.

Finally, through prayer, we seek God's peace about decisions in our hearts. Colossians 3:15 says, "Let the peace of Christ rule in your hearts, to which indeed you were called in one body; and be thankful."

Here, the word "rule" allows the peace of God to act as an umpire in our hearts. In baseball, an umpire referees the game, calls the balls and strikes, and makes the decisions on whether the ball is hit fair or foul. We must allow God's peace to act as our umpire.

Over the years, many situations have caused me to rely on this peace. When I graduated from seminary, I discerned what move God wanted us to make. I received a call from a church in South Carolina that wanted to interview me for the pastorate. After visiting and praying through it, God would not give me peace about taking that ministry. Pam gave me confirmation with her own lack of peace.

Another church called and asked if I'd consider planting a church in Atlanta. In those days, church planting was not at the forefront of young ministers' minds like it is today. Church planting wasn't even on my radar. Although we had no money and had a young child to care for, we didn't immediately dismiss this possibility.

We prayed about it. We visited the area, which seemed to have plenty of churches already. Yet, as we committed the situation to prayer, we began to have a peace about going there. I imagined the area's homes and neighborhoods in my mind. God placed a burden on my heart for these people. Within weeks, we developed a lasting peace and made the decision to start the church.

It was a great decision for us. We not only planted that church, but also two others which still stand today. In those nine years, God blessed our family as well. I believe that through faith with the small things (starting out with just Pam, our one-year-old son and me), God led us to greater future responsibility.

In summary, our relationship with God is key to discerning His will. We must pray often, saturate ourselves with God's Word, and open ourselves with humility to His guidance even before it's given.

Realize the Nature of the Battle

The battle for Jericho was special. The Israelites fought for land already given them by God. But, in the first battle, God made a statement. God showed the Israelites that this war was spiritual and that He is all-powerful. He was their rescuer.

As I stated in chapter 5, we're in a spiritual battle. In this particular battle, there were two specific characteristics. First, the odds were overwhelming. Second, God intervened in a very direct and unusual way. He often wants to help us fight battles, because it's through tough battles that we grow and become stronger in our faith. Sometimes He wants to step in to demonstrate His power and show us that He is our rescuer. A great example of this is our salvation experience.

As we grow in Christ, God helps us through our spiritual battles. He comforts us when we are dismayed. He delivers us from temptation—although we usually feel the pain of it. God encourages and guides us through the trials of life. However, the initial battle of salvation is all His to win.

Everyone has their own unique set of circumstances before salvation. Even though it's our responsibility to claim what Christ has done, it's the Father who initiated our salvation, Christ who paid for our salvation and the Holy Spirit who applies our salvation. Like the battle of Jericho, our salvation shows God's great power. It demonstrates how much He loves us. Through salvation, we see that Jesus has come to rescue.

Have the Right Strategy

At first glance, the Israelites were given an irrational strategy.

> Then on the seventh day they rose early at the dawning of the day and marched around the city in the same

manner seven times; only on that day they marched around the city seven times. At the seventh time, when the priests blew the trumpets, Joshua said to the people, "Shout! For the LORD has given you the city. The city shall be under the ban, it and all that is in it belongs to the LORD; only Rahab the harlot and all who are with her in the house shall live, because she hid the messengers whom we sent. But as for you, only keep yourselves from the things under the ban, so that you do not covet *them* and take some of the things under the ban, and make the camp of Israel accursed and bring trouble on it. But all the silver and gold and articles of bronze and iron are holy to the LORD; they shall go into the treasury of the LORD." So the people shouted, and *priests* blew the trumpets; and when the people heard the sound of the trumpet, the people shouted with a great shout and the wall fell down flat, so that the people went up into the city, every man straight ahead, and they took the city. (Josh. 6:15–20)

Doing the right thing, from the right heart, still requires the right strategy. The Israelites were to march around the city once each day for six days. On the seventh day, they were to march around the city seven times. They had no training, few resources and puzzling instructions. God knew, however, that (besides Himself) fear was the only thing the Israelites had going for them. For years, the Canaanites heard about the parting of a sea, bread from heaven and water coming from a rock, so they knew they were dealing with a very powerful God.

Can you imagine the fear and dread in the city of Jericho? The increasing anticipation and mystery, as the Jews marched around the city each day? When the time was right, God performed the miracle and the victory was won. What did the

Israelites do? They heard from God, followed orders and went forth with courageous faith.

Can you think of other puzzling strategies God planned? Take our salvation, for example. If we made a salvation plan, would we develop the one God gave us? Doesn't it make more sense to have salvation based on our merit or the works we do? Every other religion in the world is based on works, which itself is the word "do." One must *do* something to earn salvation or good standing with God.

When I was a child, I thought being good was the way to heaven. I remember sitting in a Sunday school class at age twelve hearing the teacher speak of God's grace.

I finally asked, "You mean all I have to do to go to heaven is receive Christ? I don't have to be good or do good things?"

He replied, "That's right, Dwayne; it's all about what Jesus did for you on the cross."

I immediately turned to my classmates, thinking they would be shocked. It sure sounded like false doctrine to me. However, all nodded in agreement, wondering how I didn't already realize this. I went home and asked my parents, thinking they would never let me go back to *that* church again. But my parents told me it was true! Salvation comes through God's grace by what Christ did for me on the cross. Wow! Talk about spiritual vertigo!

It took me quite a while to reconcile my thoughts on the subject. It did not make sense. How could a person live a good life by my standards and still receive judgment? Meanwhile, a bad person could confess Christ on his deathbed and go to heaven? How? Because Christianity is defined by one word—*done*. All that needed to be done for salvation was done. Ephesians 2:8–9 says, "For by grace you have been saved through faith; and that not of yourselves, *it is* the gift of God; not as a result of works, so that no one may boast."

If I worked for my own salvation, I could then boast about it, which would lead to self-worship. When I humbled myself before the cross, I acknowledged that I could not save myself. I needed a savior. I became a God worshiper rather than a self-worshiper.

God always has the answers. He always knows where we should go and how to get there. Not only should we pray for God's guidance on where to go, but also on how to get there. The journey is as important as the destination. God's strategies for victory are sometimes foreign to us, while other times He gives us guidelines that make more sense to the human mind.

For example, if you want to be a great Christian, there are activities that will lead you to that end. You need to make the Bible—and its study—a part of your everyday life. You need to be involved in a church where you can serve (1) by helping others grow *inside* the church and (2) by ministering to the world *outside* the church. You must pray consistently, asking for God's help with adversity and spiritual warfare. You must share your faith. All of these things are catalysts for achieving your goal.

What does God want you to do? How will God get you there? What's your next step?

March from the Place of Victory

> They utterly destroyed everything in the city, both man and woman, young and old, and ox and sheep and donkey, with the edge of the sword.

Joshua said to the two men who had spied out the land, "Go into the harlot's house and bring the woman and all she has out of there, as you have sworn to her." So the young men who were spies went in and brought out Rahab and her father and her mother and her brothers and all she had; they also brought out all her relatives and placed them outside the camp of Israel. They burned the city with fire, and all that was in it. Only the silver and gold, and articles of bronze and iron, they put into the treasury of the house of the LORD. However, Rahab the harlot and her father's household and all she had, Joshua spared; and she has lived in the midst of Israel to this day, for she hid the messengers whom Joshua sent to spy out Jericho.

Then Joshua made them take an oath at that time, saying, "Cursed before the LORD is the man who rises up and builds this city Jericho; with *the loss of* his first-born he shall lay its foundation, and with *the loss of* his youngest son he shall set up its gates." So the LORD was with Joshua, and his fame was in all the land. (Josh. 6:21–27)

Why did God punish the Canaanites so severely? The battle in Canaan had a twofold purpose. In order to inherit the land, Israel first had to fight for it, which enabled them to both grow as a nation and appreciate their God-given inheritance. It also allowed God to use them to punish the evil in Canaan.

The Canaanite society was one of the most wicked and depraved in history. They sacrificed babies on altars, and debauchery was rampant. They created gods to suit their self-centered lifestyle.

God gave them forty years to repent (plus seven additional days), but they didn't. Not only was the city of Jericho destroyed but, as promised, God also ensured nothing was ever built on that site again. To this day, few of the city's ruins remain.

Even in wrath, God remembered mercy. Rahab, the harlot, hid the men who went in to spy out the land before the invasion of Israel. In response to her faith, God spared her and her family. "By faith the walls of Jericho fell down after they had been encircled for seven days. By faith Rahab the harlot did not perish along with those who were disobedient, after she had welcomed the spies in peace" (Heb. 11:30–31).

None of us deserves God's grace. But God, in His infinite love, willingly gives it. In difficult times, what we see, hear or experience makes no sense. When we can't see the whole truth, we still know God is true. When faced with great odds, we know the God of grace is in our corner.

Knowing there is a blessing—a payoff—at the end helps greatly. We all want the trophy at the end of the race. In their book *The Millennials*, Jess and Thom Rainer say 96 percent of young people ages fourteen to thirty-four want their lives to make a difference.[4]

For the Israelites, the payoff was achieving their home in the Promised Land. For the businessperson, it might be closing a big deal. For the athlete, it might be winning a game or tournament. For Christians, the trophy should be making a difference in people's lives and bringing glory to Christ's name.

Few people want to waste their time, much less waste their lives. A leader casts vision and reveals goals and strategies. Followers, on the other hand, buy into that vision, believing the leader and the endeavor will make a difference in their lives. When Jesus called His disciples, He asked them to leave their nets behind, and He would make them fishers of men. They believed in Jesus' vision and wanted to go where He promised to take them.

Many of us feel our lives are of little consequence, little result. We rarely realize their full impact. There is one such story about sixteenth century pastor and author Matthew Henry, who died believing his ministry had failed. Today his Bible commentary is probably the most read in American history.

You may teach a small class at church. You may pastor a small country church. Perhaps you're a missionary who has failed to produce a convert to Christianity in the past five years (if you do missions in a Muslim country, that is not unusual, by the way). So where is the payoff? Let's look at the story of one Sunday school teacher.

Edward Kimball started a Sunday school class for boys in his neighborhood. One of the young men he led to Christ was Dwight L. Moody, who went on to become one of the most effective evangelists of the nineteenth century.

In his trips to England, Moody became close friends with F.B. Meyer, the pastor of Christ Church in London. Meyer's heart was set on fire and his ministry revitalized under Moody's preaching. Meyer, in turn, led J. Wilbur Chapman to Christ. Chapman was a pastor, author, teacher and leader of an organization that led Billy Sunday to Christ. Many consider Sunday the leading American evangelist of his day.

Sunday was invited to Montreat, North Carolina to preach a series of worship services. The week went so well that the members wanted to extend the series for another week. Sunday had other engagements and recommended evangelist Mordecai Ham. That week, a young man came to Christ under Ham's preaching—a young man who went on to become the leading evangelist in modern history. His name was Billy Graham.[5] It all started with one Sunday school teacher. Edward Kimball never knew his ministry would result in millions of people being led to Christ.

You may feel the odds are stacked against you; but with your life firmly in God's hands, there are no odds to beat. You and I fight *from* a place of victory, not *to* a place of victory.

Discussion Questions

1. How have you been able to discern God's will in your life?
2. As you seek to do God's will, what do you feel are your obstacles?
3. What is your strategy for growing into a consistent, dynamic Christian?
4. What is keeping you from becoming all you can be in Christ?

10

The Courage to Face Ourselves

Our church hosts a 5K run each Memorial Day weekend. Recently, I watched the race and was amazed at some of the runners. Some ran a 3.1-mile trial just to warm up. Then, after resting only a few minutes, they ran the actual race and competed well.

For the experienced runners, I suppose our 5K race is rather easy. There are no hills or obstacles on the course, and plenty of people are there to cheer you on. I think all of us would prefer life's race to be that easy. We could build spiritual muscle through Bible reading, prayer and worship and run the race with Christ unhindered.

I compare our Christian race to running a marathon in a jungle filled with hills to climb, trees to negotiate and wild animals to avoid. Can you imagine running a race while dodging rhinos and hearing the roar of lions in the brush? We face opposition and obstacles just as daunting.

Like Jacob of the Bible, we wrestle against the will of an almighty God and we battle the fiery darts of Satan. But sometimes the final—and greatest—hurdle is us. We need courage to face ourselves. Cartoon character Charlie Brown (another great theologian) once said, "We have spotted the enemy and he is us."[1]

Joshua 7 tells the story of a failed Israelite battle. Prior to this, God had promised to be with Joshua and the Israelites. He had even performed one of His greatest miracles when the walls of Jericho fell. But in this next battle, God appeared to renege on His promises when the Israelites were defeated by a small band of people at an outpost known as Ai.

> The men of Ai struck down about thirty-six of their men, and pursued them from the gate as far as Shebarim and struck them down on the descent, so the hearts of the people melted and became as water.
>
> Then Joshua tore his clothes and fell to the earth on his face before the ark of the LORD until the evening, *both* he and the elders of Israel; and they put dust on their heads. Joshua said, "Alas, O Lord GOD, why did You ever bring this people over the Jordan, *only* to deliver us into the hand of the Amorites, to destroy us? If only we had been willing to dwell beyond the Jordan! O Lord, what can I say since Israel has turned *their* back before their enemies? For the Canaanites and all the inhabitants of the land will hear of it, and they will surround us and cut off our name from the earth. And what will You do for Your great name?" (7:5–9)

Joshua was having quite the pity party. He was busy blaming God for the failures. It was time to ask questions. He was just asking the *wrong* questions.

What are the right questions when we hit a wall? We see three in this passage:

1. Who is the real hero?
2. What do I really want?
3. How do I solve the problem?

Who Is the Real Hero?

Ai was a small town of about twelve thousand.[2] It was the outpost of Bethel, a nearby larger city. The men of Ai killed thirty-six Israelites and won the battle. Previously, Israel had been successful, because God had intervened and showed them the way. Consequently, they were the talk of the town and the Israelites felt invincible. They were heroes in their own minds.

But after Israel's defeat at Ai, Joshua experienced a bout of spiritual vertigo. He had trusted the promises and character of God—and it ended in disaster.

Notice that Joshua asked God three questions:

1. Why did You even bring us here? (Josh. 7:7)
2. Why did we have to run from our enemies in shame and defeat? (7: 8) (How embarrassing!)
3. Why did You embarrass Yourself? (7: 9)

Rather than ask God why *He* failed, Joshua should have asked why *Israel* failed. Again, what we see, hear and experience may be the truth, but it's not the whole truth. We can't blame God for our failures and defeats. We must look elsewhere, even within ourselves. Before the first battle, Joshua prayed and consulted the Lord. Overconfident from the victory at Jericho, Joshua sought the advice of his spies instead of consulting with God and made his own decisions at the Battle of Ai.

> Now Joshua sent men from Jericho to Ai, which is near Beth-aven, east of Bethel, and said to them, "Go up and spy out the land." So the men went up and spied out Ai. They returned to Joshua and said to him, "Do not let all the people go up; *only* about two or three thousand men need go up to Ai; do not make all the people toil up there, for they are few" (Josh. 7:2–3)

God definitely was not part of this equation.

Success can lead down a path to failure. When we're fearful and uncertain, we consult the Lord. Quite often, we humble ourselves before the Lord, admitting our circumstances are overwhelming. But once we get a victory or two under our belts, we become self-confident.

This reminds me of the story of the mouse who was afraid to go over a long bridge. An elephant came by and assured him of the bridge's safety, but the helpless mouse was still afraid because the drop into the ravine was great.

The elephant said, "Why don't you jump on my back and I'll ride you over?" Reluctantly, the mouse agreed. As they crossed, the elephant's massive weight shook and rocked the old bridge.

Once safely across, the mouse said with confidence, "Wow, we really shook that bridge!"

Like the mouse, we attribute great achievements to our own might rather than to God. Historically, college football teams struggle to win two big games in successive weeks. One week the team looks like they could compete with the pros, the next they look like a local peewee football team could beat them. Most college players still lack maturity or play with too much emotionality. But we're Christians! Shouldn't it be different for us?

The loss at Ai revealed that Israel looked to their own strength, not God's. They were heroes and legends in their own hearts and minds, an unstoppable force and the envy of Canaan. When the Israelites witnessed the walls of Jericho fall, they knew that God was with them. They felt invincible. They thought, "No need to consult God on little ole Ai. We can handle it."

Several years ago, our church decided to build a $14 million auditorium. To give you some background, we felt like the Israelites after Jericho. For seven years, God had intervened in our church and exceeded our prayers and expectations. Every ministry we started went beyond any goal set. Each year, we received 10 to 15 percent more offerings than expenditures. The church grew from five hundred to two thousand worshipers and we averaged over 250 baptisms each year. Furthermore, every one of our capital stewardship programs exceeded our goals.

Then we found ourselves faced with great challenges. We set a pledge goal of $8.5 million for a new facility. I remember well that some staff members predicted we would far exceed the $14 million total cost. Confidence ran very high—even with broad-based participation, few considered the need for sacrificial commitment. However, the pledged total fell significantly short and caused us to step back from the project. As I look back, the only surprise is that seven years passed before overconfidence took its toll. That alone says many positive things about our church.

I wish these were isolated incidents in my life, but I fight them every day. Our last Easter service had near-record attendance and record decisions for Christ. The following Saturday night, as I looked over Sunday's message, I suddenly realized I had failed to pray for the service. I mean, I prayed but not like I did for Easter. I was still basking in the success of the previous week.

Success is often followed by a proud heart. Like the mouse on the elephant's back, somehow we can't help thinking we shook the bridge. Lord, save us from the sin of presumption! As Tim Keller said, "Our hearts are an idol factory."[3] The most popular idol is ourselves. Like King Saul said to Samuel, "Bless me now that the people will follow" (see 1 Sam. 15:17–30). Luke 9:46 says of Jesus' disciples: "An argument started among them as to which of them might be the greatest." It must have been like a Muhammad Ali convention! The problem the Israelites faced was confusion with hero worship. They thought they, not God, were the hero.

We must ask ourselves, "Who do we really want to be our hero?" "Who do we worship?" "Can God afford to bless us, or will His blessings return us to self-worship?" If God is our hero, then we won't worry about our own success. We won't boast of our victories. We will pray about the coming battles or the next challenge, regardless of the last one's outcome.

What Do I Really Want?

The second question we must ask when examining ourselves concerns our true desires. In Mark 10:46–52, we read the story of Bartimaeus, a blind man Jesus passed on a roadside. Scripture says he cried out to Jesus for help. When Jesus didn't respond, the disciples rebuked the man. That made Bartimaeus cry even louder. Jesus finally turned to him and asked, "What do you want Me to do for you?" (10:50).

Here is the question for our hearts: What do we really want? An answer to prayer? Financial gain? Success? Recognition? To be loved? To glorify Christ?

As our story continues, Joshua 7 tells us the *real* reason for the defeat at Ai: there was sin in the camp. The first verse of the chapter indicates, however, that because he failed to consult the Lord previously, Joshua wasn't aware of the sin. God revealed that problem to Joshua and the reason for Israel's defeat.

So the LORD said to Joshua, "Rise up! Why is it that you have fallen on your face? Israel has sinned, and they have also transgressed My covenant which I commanded them. And they have even taken some of the things under the ban and have both stolen and deceived. Moreover, they have also put *them* among their own things. Therefore the sons of Israel cannot stand before their enemies; they turn *their* backs before their enemies, for they have become accursed. I will not be with you anymore unless you destroy the things under the ban from your midst. Rise up! Consecrate the people and say, 'Consecrate yourselves for tomorrow, for thus the LORD, the God of Israel, has said, "There are things under the ban in your midst, O Israel. You cannot stand before your enemies until you have removed the things under the ban from your midst." In the morning then you shall come near by your tribes. And it shall be that the tribe which the LORD takes *by lot* shall come near by families, and the family which the LORD takes shall come near by households, and the household which the LORD takes shall come near man by man. It shall be that the one who is taken with the things under the ban shall be burned with fire, he and all that belongs to him, because he has transgressed the covenant of the LORD, and because he has committed a disgraceful thing in Israel.'" (Josh. 7:10–15)

Someone stole from the spoils of victory. They kept part of the riches for themselves. They coveted God's possessions; and until they dealt with their sin, God would not bless Israel. This moved Joshua to action.

So Joshua arose early in the morning and brought Israel near by tribes, and the tribe of Judah was taken. He brought the family of Judah near, and he took the family

> of the Zerahites; and he brought the family of the Zer-
> ahites near man by man, and Zabdi was taken. He
> brought his household near man by man; and Achan,
> son of Carmi, son of Zabdi, son of Zerah, from the tribe
> of Judah, was taken. Then Joshua said to Achan, "My
> son, I implore you, give glory to the LORD, the God of
> Israel, and give praise to Him; and tell me now what
> you have done. Do not hide it from me." (7:16–19)

Under Old Testament law, the first battle spoils belonged to the Lord as a first fruit offering. In ensuing battles, the spoils belonged to Israel. God only took a portion because the first fruits were holy. In Joshua 7:21, we see that Achan coveted.

> So Achan answered Joshua and said, "Truly, I have
> sinned against the LORD, the God of Israel, and this
> is what I did: when I saw among the spoil a beautiful
> mantle from Shinar and two hundred shekels of silver
> and a bar of gold fifty shekels in weight, then I coveted
> them and took them; and behold, they are concealed
> in the earth inside my tent with the silver underneath
> it." (Josh. 7:20–21)

This classical Hebrew word for "covet" means "a strong desire," the desire for things created above the Creator.[4] It means wanting something too much. How much is too much? Anything we desire more than we desire God is too much.

Some describe the Ten Commandments as two lead commands sandwiched around eight supporting commands. Read this way, the Ten Commandments warn against idol worship. The first commandment reads, "You shall have no other gods before me." The last reads, "You shall not covet . . . " The first and last are about idolatry while the middle eight describe the substance of that idolatry. Ron Dunn comments, "The sin of

Achan is taking that which belongs to God, which has been dedicated to God, and using it for ourselves."[5]

What is your idol? What do you desire more than God? Where do you struggle? We may each dig deep into our hearts to find the source of our idolatry.

There's a difference between a surface idol and a soul idol. A surface idol is what you and others can see. The soul idol is the source. It's the motive underneath the surface idol. For example, a couple went to a counselor with their marital problems. The husband told the counselor that his wife had many problems, including wanting to spend everything he made. The wife chimed in to accuse her husband of being a miser who wanted to spend nothing.

After several sessions, the counselor explained that both worshiped the same surface idol: money. They just loved and trusted it in different ways because of their unique inner needs. He needed security. He found it in money, and was therefore afraid to spend it. She, on the other hand, needed to feel significant. She fed that idol when she bought nice things for herself in order to impress her friends. Husband and wife had the same surface idol, but very different soul idols.

What do you place before God? Why do you do it? Your surface idol points to your soul idol; then the soul idol defines your life. It becomes your defining voice, telling you who you really are.

It could be a parent telling a child, "You'll never amount to anything" or a teacher calling a student "stupid." On the more positive side, if someone in church said you have a beautiful voice, you'd simply take it as a compliment. But if your favorite recording artist told you that your voice was great, that comment could define your life. You could very well spend the rest of your life trying to live up to that comment.

I recall an after-church dessert at the local Shoney's restaurant one evening following a great worship service. My pastor, Bill Ricketts, came by our table with guest evangelist Mike Gilchrist. Along with them were two friends of mine who were fortunate enough to accompany these great preachers to dinner. One of my friends overheard a comment Pastor Ricketts made about me to Reverend Gilchrist. Bill turned to Mike and said, "That young man is a real soul winner." I didn't know I was a real soul winner. But since that night, I've spent my life trying, in every way, to live up to that compliment. It helped define my life. Who or what defines yours?

It's difficult to face ourselves. I know we all struggle between a God-honoring life and wanting personal honor. I remember when we planted that church in Atlanta. In the first ten months, I didn't have a single discouraging day—quite an accomplishment if you knew me. We started the church with two people and it very quickly grew to a hundred.

I look back, however, to one particular Sunday morning in September. I expected a huge attendance increase that fall and I felt we might take the church to the next level. On that Sunday, however, the turnout was low—and I was low. For the first time in ten months, I felt genuinely discouraged. Self-doubts and fear struck me that day. What if God wasn't in this? What if He didn't bless us? Is there something wrong in my life?

To this day, I don't know the cause for those weeks of poor attendance and mediocre ministry. I do know, however, that it humbled me. Through self-examination, God revealed that I had become prideful in the church's accomplishments. Our growth was the topic of conversation amongst denominational leaders. A magazine even featured my story! I became known among my peers. I felt pressure to perform. I wanted to exceed what we had done the previous year. I didn't want to lose my notoriety or influence. In short, I concerned myself more with my own recognition and reputation than with Christ's. My fear of failure began to define my life.

So what's your problem? I know we get tired of introspection. I hate it. I want to be encouraging. However, failure is never God's fault. It may not be your fault. Maybe it's the economy, your environment, a family member. If so, it's temporary. But if it's you, the hand of God will never be at work until you deal with the obstacle. Achan had greed and covetousness. I have had my struggles with ego. Can you face yourself today?

How Do I Solve the Problem?

The third step in self-discovery involves a solution. As stated above, before solving a problem you must first define it. Joshua blamed God and once his rant finished, God told him the reason for the setback.

> Israel has sinned, and they have also transgressed My covenant which I commanded them. And they have even taken some of the things under the ban and have both stolen and deceived. Moreover, they have also put *them* among their own things. Therefore the sons of Israel cannot stand before their enemies; they turn *their* backs before their enemies, for they have become accursed. I will not be with you anymore unless you destroy the things under the ban from your midst. (Josh. 7:11–12)

Achan's sin affected everyone, including the men who were killed in battle. Basically, God said, "I won't help you if you allow sin in your camp. Deal with the situation."

I love the Old Testament story from Second Kings 6 about the axe head that floated. Elisha and his school of prophets began to build a place to live. As they cut down trees, one of the prophet's axe heads slipped off and fell into the water. The prophet cried in 6:5, "Alas, my master! For it was borrowed." The passage continues in verses 6 and 7, "Then the man of God said, 'Where did it fall?' And when he showed him the place, he cut off a stick and threw *it* in there and made the iron float. He said, 'Take it up for yourself.' So he put out his hand and took it."

Note the first question Elisha asked was, "Where did it fall?" The late pastor and evangelist Stephen Olford said, "The place of departure is the place of recovery."[6] Wherever we left God's will or first sinned—and the hand of God left our life—is the place of recovery. What's the problem? Why the setback? Where did you fall? Please be honest with yourself. Again, I know introspection is tough but the alternative is worse. As I stated, you must reconcile with the real reason God hasn't blessed you, or you'll inevitably blame God. That will hurt your walk with God and spiral you back into spiritual vertigo.

Once you define the problem, you must strategize how to solve it. God gave Joshua the next steps.

> Rise up! Consecrate the people and say, "Consecrate yourselves for tomorrow, for thus the LORD, the God of Israel, has said, 'There are things under the ban in your midst, O Israel. You cannot stand before your enemies until you have removed the things under the ban from

your midst.' In the morning then you shall come near by your tribes. And it shall be that the tribe which the Lord takes *by lot* shall come near by families, and the family which the Lord takes shall come near by households, and the household which the Lord takes shall come near man by man. It shall be that the one who is taken with the things under the ban shall be burned with fire, he and all that belongs to him, because he has transgressed the covenant of the Lord, and because he has committed a disgraceful thing in Israel." (Josh. 7:13–15)

The strategy always fits the situation. In this case, the strategy involves repentance and restoration with God. In Joshua, we see death was the only way to deal with sin. Achan confessed his sin in Joshua 7:20. The Israelites stoned him and his family (those who had knowledge of the stolen treasure) to death (see 7:25–26).

This may seem cruel and vindictive. However, please keep in mind we're dealing with a situation that occurred under the law before the grace of the cross. Grace doesn't change how God feels about sin, but it does change how He deals with it. Also, think about what Achan's sin cost. Thirty-six men died in the battle for Ai. That means thirty-six wives lost their husbands. Many more children lost their dads. The lost battle made the enemy confident. The loss hurt Joshua's leadership. The loss disgraced God's name.

Achan's sin affected many, just as our sinful actions adversely affect those around us. Consider the drunk driver who hurts or kills others, the addict who saddens their whole family, the rebellious son who breaks his parents' hearts (often passing his rebellion on to his children). The Bible teaches that the church is one body. When one part of the body lives in unrepentant sin, the entire body of Christ is affected.

Here, we see the only way to deal with sin is death. This again is illustrated in Second Kings 6 when the prophet told Elisha that his axe head fell into the water. Elisha broke a branch and tested it on the spot where the prophet said it fell. The wooden branch in the story symbolizes the cross. They applied the branch at the place of loss. When Jesus died on the cross, the cross itself was applied to our lost condition. His death is the solution for our sin because Christ died in our place. He took our sin from us to set us free. We must destroy the idol in our hearts, see it for what it is, and allow God's voice to define who we are.

What Now?

Applied practically, death is the only way to solve the sins of our past. If you haven't received Christ, that's your first step. "But as many as received Him, to them He gave the right to become children of God, *even* to those who believe in His name" (John 1:12). Christ applies His cross to every sin you ever commit. If you're already a believer and sin is the cause of your missed opportunity, the answer is still to apply the cross to your life. We often call this process "dying to self."

Galatians 2:20 teaches, "I have been crucified with Christ; and it is no longer I who live, but Christ lives in me; and the *life* which I now live in the flesh I live by faith in the Son of God, who loved me and gave Himself up for me." Ephesians 4:21–23 says, "You have heard Him and have been taught in Him, . . . that, in reference to your former manner of life, you lay aside the old self, which is being corrupted in accordance with the lusts of deceit, and that you be renewed in the spirit of your mind."

We reject the old being with its sinfulness the moment we receive Christ. However, putting that into action is a daily undertaking. The Christian life is a process of becoming who we really are and living like it. It's destroying the old gods and idols to embrace the one *true* God. It's no longer being your own hero or your own savior.

As long as I hold onto my idols, I can't break through to receive all God has for me. I won't be able to accelerate with courageous faith. If I'm my own god or the hero of my life, then stepping out in faith is very risky. There's too much to lose. How can I be sure I have the talent or strength to meet the challenge?

I heard a pastor tell a story about a young woman called to the mission field. At sixteen, she attended a missions conference and felt called to spend her life in Asia. She later learned that female missionaries were required to be married. She prayed, "Lord, I take my own hands completely off my life. The only thing I ask of you is to provide for me a husband."

Years passed. She went to college and studied missions. She even attended missionary school (similar to seminary today). The night before graduation, she sat alone in her room. Still no husband. Not even a prospect. She became angry with God. She vented long and hard to God for not doing His part as she sacrificed for Him. God spoke to her heart. She had envisioned a heroic, sacrificial and admired life for herself. She had surrendered to a life she felt would be most pleasing to God. Thereafter, God would love her more and hold her in high esteem. In so doing, she placed God under obligation—the obligation to serve her by providing a husband. She never really took her hands off her own life. That night, she made the decision to do just that and it set her free. Christ became the master. She became the servant.[7]

Think about it: If this dedicated, sacrificial young woman failed to take her hands off her own life, what about me? What about you? Have we really taken our hands off our life and fully surrendered to Christ? Is He the true object of our faith and worship?

Yes, self-examination is difficult but necessary. It teaches real courage—the courage to face ourselves.

Discussion Questions

1. Think about a time when you felt faced with defeat. Who was the real hero of the situation? Who would receive the glory if you succeeded?
2. If you could ask God for only one thing (with a guarantee of receiving it), what would it be? What does this say about your deepest desire?
3. What does the word "repentance" mean to you? How do you feel when someone suggests you need repentance for your sin or actions?
4. Have you taken your hands off your life? What does/would that look like?

11

Moving Forward in Uncertainty

It's wonderful to know God's will. It's great to know for certain what our next move should be. It's desirable. It's a good thing. But as I begin this chapter, I want to ask a few questions. Do you feel you *must* know God's will before you act? If the answer is yes, does this make you feel restricted?

The reason for my question is my long-held belief that God wants me to do His will, and as such, He is more than anxious to reveal it. As a pastor, I find this both encouraging and stressful. The logic goes: Since I'm a man of God, I should know His will for both my life and the church. Therefore, people often believe as a man of God, I never miss His will and subsequently make the right decisions and that if I make the right (God-led) decisions, all should go well with no problems.

As the family leader, many dads face the same stress. The function of a leader is to make good decisions, so some dads think, "I can't afford to mess up, or my family won't admire and respect me." This type of fear can paralyze our lives.

These fears contribute to life's "what ifs." What if I invest in this business and it fails? My wife will think I'm an inept provider. What if the economy tanks again? What if the wrong crowd at college influences my child? What if I begin teaching in church and fail? What if I take a risk and lose my job? The list goes on.

The idea that we must be certain of a positive outcome before we act is both unrealistic and unscriptural. In the book of Esther, for example, Esther is about to approach the king with Haman's scheme to destroy the Jews. She knows that a misstep could cost her life.

In Esther 4:16 she says, "Go, assemble all the Jews who are found in Susa, and fast for me; do not eat or drink for three days, night or day. I and my maidens also will fast in the same way. And thus I will go in to the king, which is not according to the law; and if I perish, I perish." She seems to know what she must do, but realizes much risk is involved.

In Daniel 3, there is the familiar story of Meshach, Shadrach and Abednego, who were cast into a fiery furnace. When given the option to worship the gold statue of King Nebuchadnezzar or perish in the fire, they replied, "If it be *so*, our God whom we serve is able to deliver us from the furnace of blazing fire; and He will deliver us out of your hand, O king. But *even* if *He does* not, let it be known to you, O king, that we are not going to serve your gods or worship the golden image that you have set up" (3:17–18). The phrase "even if he does not" exhibits great courage and uncertainty on their part. Like Esther, they went to do what God wanted, unsure of the outcome.

Finally, one of my favorite Bible characters had similar doubts. Caleb was a hero of Kadesh-barnea. He was one of twelve spies Moses sent into the Promised Land (see Num. 13-14). Ten of the spies came back with discouraging reports and placed fear in the hearts of the people; they talked of for- tified cities and a land of giants. The Bible says they made the heart of the people melt (see Josh. 14:8). Joshua and Caleb tried to calm the people. In Numbers 13:30, Caleb said, "We should by all means go up and take possession of it, for we will surely overcome it." But the people of Israel decided to follow the report of the ten spies and rebelled against the Lord. God promised judgment on the people by disallowing that generation to enter the Promised Land.

In Joshua 14, Caleb claimed the property God promised him.

> Then the sons of Judah drew near to Joshua in Gilgal, and Caleb the son of Jephunneh the Kenizzite said to him, "You know the word which the LORD spoke to Moses the man of God concerning you and me in Kadesh-barnea. I was forty years old when Moses the servant of the LORD sent me from Kadesh-barnea to spy out the land, and I brought word back to him as it was in my heart. Nevertheless my brethren who went up with me made the heart of the people melt with fear; but I followed the LORD my God fully. So Moses swore on that day, saying, 'Surely the land on which your foot has trodden will be an inheritance to you and to your children forever, because you have followed the LORD my God fully.' Now behold, the LORD has let me live, just as He spoke, these forty-five years, from the time that the LORD spoke this word to Moses, when Israel walked in the wilderness; and now behold, I am eighty-five years old today. I am still as strong today as I was in the day Moses sent me; as my strength was then, so my strength is now, for war and for going out and coming in. Now then, give me this hill country about which the LORD spoke on that day, for you heard on that day that Anakim were there, with great fortified cities; **perhaps** the LORD will be with me, and I will drive them out as the LORD has spoken." (Josh. 14:6–12)

The word "perhaps" in verse 12 has always troubled me. What does it mean? Is this doubt? Is it ever acceptable to doubt? What things are certain? How do I handle that which is uncertain?

I want to focus on four points in this passage that help free us from the tyranny of thinking that absolute certainty is necessary to move forward in faith:

1. Some things are clear.
2. Some things are not clear.
3. Some risk is good.
4. Some response is needed.

Some Things Are Clear

As Caleb looks to take his inheritance, a few things are clear to him. God was with Joshua as He was with Moses and no one could stand before the nation of Israel (see 1:5). The land of Hebron was his (see 14:9). Caleb didn't doubt they could capture Hebron, but was aware of the possibility that he might not live to enjoy the victory.

There are things we can be certain of, as well. When God makes promises, we can have assurance He will deliver.

For example, we can be sure of our salvation. If we call on God to save us, He will (see Rom. 10:13). We can be sure there is a heaven for us to inherit (see John 14:1–3). There are over six thousand promises in the Bible. We can be sure of all of them.

One of the more obscure promises concerns the giants in Caleb's life. The sons of the Anakim were the same as the giants from Gath (see Josh. 11:22). There is a history in the Bible concerning these giants (see Num. 13:33). God promised that not one of them could stand before the armies of Israel (see Josh. 11).

Hear, O Israel! You are crossing over the Jordan today to go in to dispossess nations greater and mightier than you, great cities fortified to heaven, a people great and tall, the sons of the Anakim, whom you know and of whom you have heard *it said*, "Who can stand before the sons of Anak?" Know therefore today that it is the LORD your God who is crossing over before you as a consuming fire. He will destroy them and He will subdue them before you, so that you may drive them out and destroy them quickly, just as the LORD has spoken to you.(Deut. 9:1–3)

Then we find in Joshua 11:21–22, "Then Joshua came at that time and cut off the Anakim from the hill country, from Hebron, from Debir, from Anab and from all the hill country of Judah and from all the hill country of Israel. Joshua utterly destroyed them with their cities. There were no Anakim left in the land of the sons of Israel; only in Gaza, in Gath, and in Ashdod some remained."

Hundreds of years later, when David approached Goliath, he knew the giant had no chance against him because Goliath was a son of Gath, a leftover from the day of the Exodus (see 1 Sam. 17:4). God promised they would conquer the sons of Gath (see 1 Chron. 17:10). David simply claimed this promise (see 18:1).

We can be sure that all of God's promises are true. Some of these promises and certainties center on the purpose God has for our lives. Proverbs 3:5–6 teaches, "Trust in the LORD with all your heart / And do not lean on your own understanding. / In all your ways acknowledge Him, / And He will make your paths straight." Again, I refer to Jeremiah 29:11: "'For I know the plans that I have for you,' declares the LORD, 'plans for

welfare and not for calamity to give you a future and a hope.'"
What's clear about God's will?

A General Will

God's specific will for our lives is unique to every believer.
However, the general will or purpose God has for all of us is
that we live our lives for His glory. "I will say to the north, 'Give
them up!' / And to the south, 'Do not hold *them* back.' / Bring
My sons from afar / And My daughters from the ends of the
earth, / Everyone who is called by My name, / And whom I
have created for My **glory**, / Whom I have formed, even whom
I have made'" (Isa. 43:6–7).

But what is "glory"? The term can have several meanings. One
of them is to magnify something.[1] Our calling is to magnify
Christ in the world and the church. In his book *Don't Waste Your
Life,* author John Piper says when we think of magnifying something, a microscope or telescope comes to mind. A microscope
makes something small look bigger than it is in reality. God is
not small, and we can't make Him look any bigger than He is.

The second way to magnify is by using a telescope. A telescope does two things. First, it makes things seem closer and,
second, it makes the object's perspective look closer to its actual
size. When we magnify Christ, we bring Him closer to the
world and make Him bigger—a little closer to His actual size!
Our purpose on Earth is to draw others to Him. Piper goes on
to explain that if we don't magnify Him, we waste our lives.[2]

We magnify Christ by living for Him, under His lordship.
We live for Him by worshiping Him, walking with Him and
working with Him. How do we work with Him? By serving
others. As we serve in Jesus' name, we become His hands. Others

see Jesus in us. A major ingredient of our general purpose is ministry. As we serve others, we must do so with a spirit of redemption. What purpose is there in merely being nice to people, feeding them, and ministering to their emotional needs when their future lies in eternal damnation? Without eternity in mind, all our charitable works do is simply make life a little easier for people, for the few years they have on Earth. The only lasting service ministry we have is that which affects eternity.

I know you want to serve others without "an angle." You want to serve without any thoughts toward alternative reasons. I get that. We may think: "If I help this person and then share Christ with them, they'll think I only helped in order to get them to listen—to come over to my way of thinking, to put a notch in my Bible for another soul saved."

Let me challenge you to look at the situation differently. Serve them. As you minister, give money, or simply help them, do it out of a heart of ministry. Since eternity is on the line, you are doing them a far greater service by sharing Christ with them. They are not doing you a favor by listening. You are doing them a favor by sharing the greatest message of liberation and life change in the history of the world.

Through your actions, you will magnify Christ and enlighten the person spiritually, and they will perhaps become a follower of Christ. If I simply help someone without them knowing that Christ motivates me, then they think I'm a great person. In other words, I'm the one glorified.

God has the right to ask me to live for His glory, because He created me and He bought me out of sin and slavery. First Corinthians 6:20 says, "For you have been bought with a price: therefore glorify God in your body."

I heard a story about a little boy who built a model ship. It took him many weeks of meticulous work. At the end, he was very proud of his accomplishment. One day, his house was robbed and his ship stolen. For weeks, he saw nothing of the ship and thought it was lost. Then, as he walked down the street of a shopping area in his hometown, he noticed the ship in the store window at a pawnshop. He went into the store and informed the storeowner the ship belonged to him.

The owner, however, told the boy that he paid good money for the little ship; and if he wanted it, he had to buy it. The boy rushed home, broke his piggy bank, gathered up his money, ran back to the store and bought the ship. As he was walking out of the store, he held the ship in both hands, looked at it, and said, "You are twice mine. First I created you and now I bought you." Jesus both created us (see John 1:3) and bought us through His death on the cross. He is God and deserves our worship and service.

A Specific Will

God has the same general purpose for every Christian; however, He also has a specific will or purpose for each individual. I love the calling of Jeremiah because it tells me about my relationship with God.

> Now the word of the Lord came to me saying,
> "Before I **formed** you in the womb **I knew you**, And before you were born **I consecrated you; I have ap- pointed you** a prophet to the nations."
> Then I said, "Alas, Lord God!
> Behold, I do not know how to speak,
> Because I am a youth."
> But the Lord said to me,

"Do not say, 'I am a youth,'
Because everywhere I send you, you shall go,
And all that I command you, you shall speak.
"Do not be afraid of them,
For I am with you to deliver you," declares the LORD.

Then the LORD stretched out His hand and touched my mouth, and the LORD said to me,

"Behold, I have put My words in your mouth.
See, I have appointed you this day over the nations and over the kingdoms,
To pluck up and to break down,
To destroy and to overthrow, To build and to plant."

(Jer. 1:4–10)

These verses tell us that God takes the initiative in our lives. Notice it tells us that:

- God formed
- God knew
- God consecrated
- God appointed

This passage informs us that all human life is precious to God. We see this principle in Psalm 139:13–16 as well.

For You formed my inward parts;
You wove me in my mother's womb.
I will give thanks to You, for I am fearfully and wonderfully made;
Wonderful are your works,
And my soul knows it very well.
My frame was not hidden from You,
When I was made in secret,
And skillfully wrought in the depths of the earth;
Your eyes have seen my unformed substance;

And in Your book were all written
The days that were ordained *for me*,
When as yet there was not one of them.

How do we discern that plan? In chapter 7, I listed a few general principles for finding God's will through His Word. Over the years, I've compiled many checklists from numerous sermons and books that point to specifics for finding God's will. Here are a few guidelines that helped me:

- Build a strong relationship with God through church attendance, Bible reading and prayer. These are key elements in seeking God's wisdom for decisions. If you want to know God's will, the Holy Spirit must speak to you. He must give you God's wisdom and direction. The Holy Spirit speaks through relationship, and we build a relationship with God by fellowshipping with other Christians, reading His Word and praying regularly.
- Study the experiences God gave you in the past. He seldom takes us in varying directions in life. God tends to build His plan for our lives on our past experience, education, and foundational tools to obtain certain vocations or relationships. For example, if a young person feels led to take a business major in college, God will probably use this education as a platform for the future. God usually has us take our steps on the same staircase.
- Look to seasoned Christians for godly advice. What do the church leaders say about you and your life? I find this a good way to confirm God's will in my life. When I was called into ministry, trusted church leaders confirmed this in my life.

- Use wisdom from Scripture. Sometimes God gives us a verse that speaks to our specific situation. When I felt God was leading me to leave my pastorate so I could further my education in seminary, the Lord spoke to me through Proverbs 21:31: "The horse is prepared for the day of battle, / But victory belongs to the LORD." That may sound strange to you, but it helped point me in the right direction.

- Make peace in your heart. "Let the peace of Christ rule in your hearts, to which indeed you were called in one body; and be thankful" (Col. 3:15). This is the most subjective part of discerning God's will. I think, ultimately, this is what we all strive for. We want an inner tranquility and confidence that we have discerned God's will in a matter. This peace cannot contradict Scripture. It needs to be a lasting peace, not simply an emotional experience. We often need to experience this peace or confidence in the new direction for days, possibly weeks, before we move forward.

I remember my calling to become pastor of my current church. Nine years after we planted the church near Atlanta, we began to feel that perhaps God wanted us to be open to other possibilities—even though we enjoyed a wonderful ministry there with many wonderful people. In spite of the fact that the church had only been at that location for seven years, the people felt we should be open to considering a campus relocation.

Although I then hoped to stay at that church for the rest of my ministry, the thought of seven or eight more years committed to relocation and reestablishment challenged my long-term vision. Throughout this time, my wife and I began to feel a restlessness. It became more difficult to see ourselves at the church long-term. There was a slight inner turmoil in our hearts. Some may call this a "small, still inner voice."

We prayed that God would lead us to peace about either staying or going. I asked one of my mentors for his opinion. He said he preferred that we stay in Atlanta, but advised me to be open. He added that unless I had an active resume, I was not truly open.

So I put a resume together and gave it to five individuals from my list of references. A few months later, two copies of that resume came before the chairman of the pastor search committee at a church in Central Florida. When he received both of these copies in his mailbox on the same day—from two different individuals—he called me immediately.

After much prayer and three visits to Oviedo, Florida, we found ourselves awaiting the church vote one Sunday night in May. Even then, I was only about 95 percent positive this was where God wanted us to go. I had always been 100 percent certain before, so 95 percent was not very comforting. Pam, our three children and I prayed as we waited for the church to vote. We decided the vote needed to be at least 95 percent positive if we were to move. The vote came back at 99 percent! When the chairman shared the vote results, he also wanted an answer. Not until I said "yes" did I feel peace and assurance that God indeed wanted us to make the move.

Since then, I have never doubted it. I was certain, but in the midst of uncertainty—probably because of emotions. We didn't want to leave our church in Atlanta. We planted that church and loved the people. Deep within my heart, I knew the people in Atlanta needed new leadership. They had grown too dependent on us. They needed to take greater ownership. Emotions, family, finances and fears all play into decision making. Some things are certain—some things are not.

Some Things Are Uncertain

Clarity moves us to action. Ambiguity causes procrastination. But some things are not clear.

"Perhaps" is another word that bothered me for years. It contains a measure of hope, but basically means "maybe." This word doesn't make me beam with confidence. This is where our doubt sets in.

The apostle Paul went through much persecution and died for his faith. Stephen was stoned to death for preaching the gospel. How can we reconcile that with Joshua 1:8–9? "This book of the law shall not depart from your mouth, but you shall meditate on it day and night, so that you may be careful to do according to all that is written in it; for then you will make your way prosperous, and then you will have success. Have I not commanded you? Be strong and courageous! Do not tremble or be dismayed, for the LORD your God is with you wherever you go."

This verse does not teach that we will be successful every day, but rather that we can have success as a result of following God. Again, the Bible teaches us that everything works together for the good of those who follow Christ (see Rom. 8:28). The Bible does *not* teach that we'll always win our battles or that those battles will not cost something. That's why acting on faith is a major step. There is risk involved.

Webster's dictionary defines "risk" as "the possibility that something bad or unpleasant (such as an injury or a loss) will happen."[3] You and I take risks when we step out on faith because we don't know the future. We don't have a crystal ball or a time machine to help us see ahead.

"Come now, you who say, 'Today or tomorrow we will go to such and such a city, and spend a year there and engage in business and make a profit.' Yet you do not know what your life will be like tomorrow. You are *just* a vapor that appears for a little while and then vanishes away. Instead, *you ought* to say, 'If the Lord wills, we will live and also do this or that'" (James 4:13–15).

It's scary to imagine that walking with God could be risky. Yet we know there are many unexplainable things going on in our world and in our personal lives.

In 2009, Asia Bibi, a Pakistani Christian, was arrested for her faith. She found herself in an argument with some Muslim women in her village after she drank water the Muslim women had retrieved. They declared it unclean because Bibi drank from the pitcher. The dispute escalated when Bibi defended her Christian faith. Hours after the dispute, Bibi was arrested for blasphemy and was subsequently convicted. She now sits on death row.[4]

With the advancement of the terrorist group ISIS, persecution of Christians in the Middle East has reached historic levels. Are these Christians missing the will of God? Why doesn't God rescue them? If we obey God, isn't everything supposed to work out well?

On another, less dramatic note, I know a pastor who terminated the employment of a long-standing minister at his church. The employee deserved to be fired and the pastor explained the rationality of the termination. Even though the pastor's actions were justified, he suffered for them. The fallout in his church was great. We often do what is right and suffer the consequences. What gives?

One of the fallacies that play into this is a feeling that God's will is easy. That is, if we discern God's will and do it, all will go smoothly, without any problems. That's simply not true. It's not biblical. We fight a spiritual warfare battle every day.

The adversity we face tests us and places us through brokenness and change. If we follow Christ, does that mean He no longer desires to change us? Mold us? Does it mean that we no longer need growth? Does it mean that Satan is going to give us a pass?

Sometimes following Christ means jumping into the pit with the lion. Sometimes it means being alone on the battlefield facing a giant. Sometimes it means that the decisions we make bring greater hardship on us. Right decisions don't necessarily mean a nonresistant path.

Since we are fallible and cannot see the future, we take risks when we attempt new ventures. I must give myself some slack. Yes, followers must give slack as well. We must have room to fail, to make a wrong turn.

If we have no room to fail, we have no room to risk. If we have no room to risk, we'll be very reluctant to act.

Some Risk Is Good

In Joshua 14:12, Caleb says to Joshua, "Now then, give me this hill country about which the LORD spoke on that day, for you heard on that day that Anakim *were* there, with great fortified cities; perhaps the LORD will be with me, and I will drive them out as the LORD has spoken."

Risk is simply another term for stepping out on faith. Caleb knew he had to take a risk as a step of faith when he marched forward to claim his inheritance. The land of Hebron was his for the taking. However, going to battle to capture the city and its surroundings would cost the lives of many of his people, perhaps even his own life.

The risk is not in God. God is always good. He never fails; He always keeps His promises. The risk is in the task itself. Our fear is that the task may not end the way we want or envision.

Risk Tests Our Hearts

Why is risk good? First, when we step out in faith, we do so believing God will take care of us. Does this always include our version of success? If so, who are we trying to magnify? Philippians 1:21 teaches us, "For to me, to live is Christ and to die is gain."

Later in that same book, Paul wrote, "Brethren, I do not regard myself as having laid hold of *it* yet; but one thing *I do*: forgetting what *lies* behind and reaching forward to what *lies* ahead, I press on toward the goal for the prize of the upward call of God in Christ Jesus" (Phil. 3:13–14). Paul's *one thing* is Christ and to bring Him glory in all he did.

Another benefit to risk is that it brings excitement to our Christian experience. Mark Batterson said, "Faith is embracing the uncertainties of life. It is chasing the lions that cross our paths. It is recognizing a divine appointment when you see one."[5]

Risk, or stepping out in faith, brings uncertainty to life. With this uncertainty comes challenges, and challenges bring interest and excitement. Faith embraces uncertainty. It is through those doubts that our relationship with God grows and we gain confidence in Him.

The problem we often face, however, is that our human nature desires safety. The older we get, the more attractive safety becomes. Young pastors and business people often start their professional lives taking chances, stepping out in faith and attacking high-risk projects. Then, as age sets in, we shy away from those risks.

Battle weary from years of pastoral struggles, he's now content to live an easier life and simply keep his ministry. The successful businessman no longer has interest in risky pursuits. He has too much to lose. He's tired and just wants to play it safe.

Just as our salvation is safe in Christ, so are our risks. According to Proverbs 18:10, "The name of the LORD is a strong tower; / The righteous runs into it and is safe." As long as we follow Christ, nothing can happen unless He allows it to happen. This is safety. However, I don't recall the Scripture depicting Christ living a life of safety.

In his book *The Lion, the Witch and the Wardrobe*, C.S. Lewis writes, "Aslan is a lion—the Lion, the great Lion," said Mr. Beaver. "Ooh," said Susan. "I'd thought he was a man. Is he—quite safe? I shall feel rather nervous about meeting a lion." "Who said anything about safe? 'Course he isn't safe. But he's good. He's the King, I tell you."[6]

In the book, the lion is a symbol of God.[7] God is good, but He's not safe. Jesus didn't die on the cross for our sin simply to give us a safety net. He didn't spill His blood on Calvary's cross so that you and I could sit back cowering in safety. Christ did not send His indwelling Spirit only to calm us in the midst of storms.

God is a warrior. He went to battle for us on the cross. He takes us into battle every day. Sometimes we must take Him by the hand and step into the fog, the dark, the unknown. And when we are blindsided by adversity, attacked by people, persecuted by the world, or humbled before followers, we must be still and know that He is God.

He is the one who parts the sea and locks the lion's jaw. He is *still* our rescuer.

What Does God Want?

Seizing opportunity can be merely a silencing of life's fears. Let me remind you how Caleb handled his challenge.

> I was forty years old when Moses the servant of the LORD sent me from Kadesh-barnea to spy out the land, and I brought word back to him as *it was* in my heart. Nevertheless my brethren who went up with me made the heart of the people melt with fear; but I followed the LORD my God fully. So Moses swore on that day, saying "Surely the land on which your foot has trodden will be an inheritance to you and to your children forever, because you have followed the LORD my God fully." (Josh. 14:7-9)

Caleb remembered the past. He looked at his part from God's perspective gratefully. His faith stood between "no longer" and "not yet." He was able to build an untamed, courageous faith by looking at his history. Then Caleb was able to claim his inheritance, trusting God with the outcome. His faith could process what he saw, heard and experienced because it rested in God, God's Word and God's power, not on Caleb's personal dreams and expectations.

How should we respond when moved by God to step out and take a risk? I know a pastor who is considering a name change for his church. He and the staff have discussed it for months. They see all the positive reasons for it, as well as a few negative. When he recently approached the staff on the subject, he felt they had discussed it long enough and needed to make a decision.

One staff member said that he couldn't pray clearly about it because he felt it might cause problems in the church, which had already undergone some recent changes to the protest of a few. That's when the pastor made the statement, "I think we're asking the wrong question. We're asking ourselves how our people would respond. The question we should ask ourselves is, 'What does God want us to do?'"

No matter the risk, no matter the cost, no matter the work entailed, does God want you to do it or not? Most of us know the will of God. We just lack the courage to do it.

Once we discern God's will, we then must choose our fear. We could be afraid of being embarrassed, losing money, hurting our self-esteem, losing followers or temporarily failing—or we can fear missing the will of God.

Faith embraces doubt, risk and uncertainty. Mark Batterson writes, "To be certain of God means that we are uncertain in all our ways; we do not know what a day may bring forth. This generally is said with a sigh of sadness, it should be an expression of breathless expectation."[8]

Discussion Questions

1. Do you feel stressed or restricted about getting certainty in God's will before you act?
2. What are some things that are clear in your life? Are you acting on these things?
3. What is one step that you feel God wants you to take, despite the risks? What are the risks? Are those risks hindering you from discerning God's will?
4. Can you think of a circumstance in your life that required a step of faith with risk? Was the risk good for your Christian walk?

Part 4

The Course We Take

12

Right Now!

Courageous faith always expresses itself with action. I challenged you to reach into your past, place it in God's perspective, and become thankful for what He has done. I trust this caused you to be able to reach forward toward the future with clarity and faith. At some point, however, you must move to action. You must pull the trigger. The time to do *that* is now! Procrastination is one of the biggest obstacles to action. Psalm 119:60 states, "I hastened and did not delay / To keep Your commandments."

Years ago, I heard a poem that expresses our challenge.

> The bride bent with age leaned on her cane,
> Her steps uncertain need guiding
> While down the church aisle, with a worn toothless smile
> Came the groom in a wheelchair gliding
> And who is this elderly couple that wed?
> You'll find when you've closely explored it
> That this is that rare most conservative pair
> Who waited 'till they could afford it.[1]

If we don't do as God instructs us right now, we won't do it at all. We all have good intentions and I commend you for yours. I have had good intentions too: memorizing more Scripture, sharing my faith more often, starting new ministries, or simply making a phone call to a friend. However, a good intention without action never blesses anyone. Good intentions are never rewarded. We must seize our opportunity now.

In Second Timothy 4:9–22, we read the conclusion of Paul's last will and testament. Addressed to Timothy, his son in the faith, it's the last book Paul wrote before his death. We find Paul in chains in a Roman prison. Aware that these were his final months of life, he urges Timothy to come to him soon.

> **Make every effort to come to me soon**; for Demas, having loved this present world, has deserted me and gone to Thessalonica; Crescens *has gone* to Galatia, Titus to Dalmatia. Only Luke is with me. Pick up Mark and bring him with you, for he is useful to me for service. But Tychicus I have sent to Ephesus. **When you come** bring the cloak which I left at Troas with Carpus, and the books, especially the parchments. Alexander the coppersmith did me much harm; the Lord will repay him according to his deeds. Be on guard against him yourself, for he vigorously opposed our teaching.
>
> At my first defense no one supported me, but all deserted me; may it not be counted against them. But the Lord stood with me and strengthened me, so that through me the proclamation might be fully accomplished, and that all the Gentiles might hear; and I was rescued out of the lion's mouth. The Lord will rescue me from every evil deed, and will bring me safely to His heavenly kingdom; to Him *be* the glory forever and ever. Amen.
>
> Greet Prisca and Aquila, and the household of Onesiphorus. Erastus remained at Corinth, but Trophimus I

left sick at Miletus. Make every effort to **come before winter**. Eubulus greets you, also Pudens and Linus and Claudia and all the brethren.

The Lord be with your spirit. Grace be with you.

Notice the urgency of Paul's plea in verses 9, 13 and 21. He gets specific in verse 21 when he asks Timothy to come before winter. The weather would be cold, the docks would be closed and the ships would not sail. Paul knew a spring arrival would be too late. Timothy had a small window of opportunity and he had to seize it immediately.

Let me approach this chapter with three questions:

1. Why step out in faith now?
2. How do you step out in faith now?
3. Why not step out in faith now?

Why Step Out in Faith Now?

Life is Short

Recently, I experienced another milestone birthday. I now have three adult children and five grandchildren. It seems like only yesterday my children were the same age as my grandchildren today. Now my children have children. When evangelist Billy Graham, now in his nineties, was asked what surprised him most about life his answer was simply the brevity of it.

James 4:14 teaches us, "Yet you do not know what your life will be like tomorrow. You are *just* a vapor that appears for a little while and then vanishes away." Most of us can relate to feeling like life went by all too fast. Along with that brevity comes uncertainty. Hebrews 9:27 says, "It is appointed for men to die once and after this comes judgment." God knows how long our life will last, but we do not. We are not guaranteed another day.

Life Is Measured by Time

"Therefore be careful how you walk, not as unwise men but as wise, making the most of your time, because the days are evil" (Eph. 5:15–16).

Time is the most valuable possession in this life because it is limited. Unlike money, we can't manufacture more time. We each have 86,400 seconds a day. We spend those seconds every day and can save none. We either invest them or waste them each day. There are no do-overs, no mulligans, no time machines and no fountains of youth. If our time was unlimited, it would greatly decrease in value. However, it is very limited and very precious.

The saying goes, "Life is like a coin. You can spend it any way you want, but you can spend it only once." Psalm 90:12 instructs us, "So teach us to number our days, / That we may present to You a heart of wisdom."

Suppose your lifespan is eighty years. If you think of your life as a clock and you are twenty, the hour hand is at six o'clock in the morning. If you are forty, it's high noon in your life. If you have turned sixty, it is now six o'clock in the evening and the sun is beginning to set. It's a sobering thought, and depressing if you are all about living for yourself. However, if you want to make a difference, it can be a wake up call.

Your Life Has Value

The limits of time, however, give our lives intrinsic value and the founders of our faith seized every minute for the Lord.

As I read Second Timothy, I think of Timothy as a courageous church planter. I see Luke as a physician who gave up his
practice to follow Paul on the mission field and go on to write
the Gospel of Luke and the book of Acts. They were convinced
that their lives had value. They had limited time to accomplish
God's purpose for them. There was no time to waste.

Life is like a vapor in time, but it does not have to be a vapor
in value. The world's view is that "when you're dead, you're
dead." Many believe and live as though we are all merely "dust
in the wind."

However, God placed eternity in our hearts and potential
value in our lives the moment we were born.

> For You formed my inward parts;
> You wove me in my mother's womb.
> I will give thanks to You, for I am fearfully and wo
> derfully made;
> Wonderful are Your works,
> And my soul knows it very well.
> My frame was not hidden from You,
> When I was made in secret,
> *And* skillfully wrought in the depths of the earth;
> Your eyes have seen my unformed substance;
> And in Your book were all written
> The days that were ordained *for me*,
> When as yet there was not one of them. (Ps. 139:13-16)

The fall of man marred God's plan for our lives. It is through
the cross of Christ—and by His grace—that we again have
value. How valuable are we? Ephesians 2:8–9 says, "For by grace
you have been saved through faith; and that not of yourselves,
it is the gift of God; not as a result of works, so that no one
may boast."

God saves us by grace. At the moment of our salvation, the Spirit of God comes into our lives. At that moment, Ephesians 3:2 says we become stewards of God's grace. "If indeed you have heard of the stewardship of God's grace which was given to me for you." A steward is a manager of another's household or possessions.

Everything we have is from God. Our money, time, energy, family, ministry, talents and the gospel message are all from Him and are His possessions. Scripture teaches:

"The earth is the LORD's, and all it contains, / The world, and those who dwell in it" (Ps. 24:1).

"'The silver is Mine and the gold is Mine,' declares the LORD of hosts" (Hag. 2:8).

"The land, moreover, shall not be sold permanently, for the land is Mine; for you are *but* aliens and sojourners with Me" (Lev. 25:23).

God now charges us with being stewards, managers, dispensers, and conduits of His grace. God through Christ places value in our life. That value is seen in:

- **Evangelism**—"Go therefore and make disciples of all the nations, baptizing them in the name of the Father and the Son and the Holy Spirit, teaching them to observe all that I commanded you; and lo, I am with you always, even to the end of the age" (Matt. 28:19–20).

- **Missions**—"I am under obligation both to Greeks and to barbarians, both to the wise and to the foolish. So, for my part, I am eager to preach the gospel to you also who are in Rome.

For I am not ashamed of the gospel, for it is the power of God for salvation to everyone who believes, to the Jew first and also to the Greek" (Rom. 1:14–16).

- **Teaching**—"For if I preach the gospel, I have nothing to boast of, for I am under compulsion; for woe is me if I do not preach the gospel" (1 Cor. 9:16).

- **Ministry**—"So Christ himself gave the apostles, the prophets, the evangelists, the pastors and teachers, to equip his people for works of service, so that the body of Christ may be built up" (Eph. 4:11–12, NIV).

We Must Use Time Wisely

Since life is short and our lives have value, we must use our time wisely. We cannot waste it. Again, Ephesians 5:15–16 teaches us that we are to walk in wisdom. Wisdom is applied knowledge. We need the wisdom of God to discern what God wants us to do and the wisdom to do it right now.

The Old Testament characters acted on God's commands immediately. Following God's instructions, Abraham left his homeland. He didn't hesitate to go up the mountain to sacrifice Isaac. After arguing with God, Moses left to rescue the Israelites from Egypt. Elijah challenged the prophets of Baal at Mount Carmel. Eli told Samuel to listen to the voice of God and do as He instructed. The New Testament uses the word "immediately" fifty-six times, including forty-two times in the Gospels.

How Do You Step Out in Faith Now?

What are some of the areas where God wants you to act *right now*? As we look at Second Timothy 4 more closely, we find there are several areas where God wants you to move with urgency.

In Your Walk with God

Demas is a man in the New Testament who is mentioned only three times, as Bible teacher Ron Dunn pointed out.[2] The first is found in Philemon where Paul calls him my "fellow worker." He is named in the same sentence as Mark and Luke. The second time, Paul mentions him in Colossians 4, where there is no description. He just refers to him as "Demas." The last time is in Second Timothy 4:10, where Paul says that Demas has deserted him. We read "For Demas, having loved this present world, has deserted me and gone to Thessalonica; Crescens *has gone* to Galatia, Titus to Dalmatia."

It would seem that there was a digression in Demas' life. He drifted away from Paul and God. The passage doesn't say that Demas stopped following Christ. It may be he got weary of the rigors of mission work or he lost his passion for it. Perhaps he just decided to go back to Thessalonica and warm a pew in church. Maybe he had good intentions of getting involved again "one day."

What about your walk with God? Is there anything you could do right now to reignite it? Are you reading your Bible daily? Are you applying what you read to your life? What about your prayer life? Has God convicted you to wake up a few minutes earlier each morning to have meaningful time with Him? Do you do it?

Do you remember the first time God moved you to develop a dynamic prayer life? Let's just suppose it was five years ago. What if you had begun that prayer journey then? What difference do you think five years of fervent prayer would have made in your family, your country, your church, your life? This world might be a better place. For sure, your life would be in a better place.

God invites you to walk with Him. Do it now! As soon as you stop reading this chapter, pick up your Bible and read it. Pause, even now, and pray that God will bless you, become more real to you and draw closer to you. Do it now!

In a Task for God

In Second Timothy 4:11, Paul says, "Only Luke is with me." Indeed, Luke stood by him when everyone else walked away. Luke was Paul's personal physician and writer-in-residence. God called Luke for a purpose and he fulfilled that purpose. What did God call you to do? Did He call you to start a business? Did He call you to teach at your church? Did He call you to be involved in giving or in missions? It is easy to convince yourself that you will answer God's call next week or next year. Procrastination requires no courage.

One example we can identify with is dieting and exercise. Dieting is an easy decision after a large dinner. Exercise is easy to begin—next week. If you don't start now, you won't start. How many years have you planned to begin a ministry in your church? You've put it off for several years. We think that, because the world didn't cave in on us, our waiting must be alright with God. The sense of urgency has long passed.

What if Luke had that attitude and said, "I know I need to write this story about Christ (the Gospel of Luke), but I will start it next week." Luke had to discipline himself to do it. Timothy also had windows of opportunity. He needed to "come before winter," before the boats were docked. We need to act before our own winter—before the desire fades, before the talents are gone, before the opportunity is lost.

In Reconciliation with Others

Second Timothy 4:11 also says, "Pick up Mark and bring him with you, for he is useful to me for service." We can't appreciate the gravity of this verse until we explore the background. Mark was the nephew of Paul's mentor in ministry, Barnabas. Paul and Barnabas took young Mark on a missionary journey. During the trip, Mark left them and went back home.

According to Acts 15, Paul and Barnabas later had a sharp disagreement over Mark.

> After some days Paul said to Barnabas, "Let us return and visit the brethren in every city in which we proclaimed the word of the Lord, *and see* how they are." Barnabas wanted to take John, called Mark, along with them also. But Paul kept insisting that they should not take him along who had deserted them in Pamphylia and had not gone with them to the work. And there occurred such a sharp disagreement that they separated from one another, and Barnabas took Mark with him and sailed away to Cyprus. But Paul chose Silas and left, being committed by the brethren to the grace of the Lord. (Acts 15:36–40)

The argument was so severe that it caused a rift in their relationship and a split in their ministry. The Bible doesn't tell us how Mark reacted to the news. I can only imagine that Mark asked Barnabas, "Where is Paul? Why are we splitting up? What happened? Was it me?" I'm sure Barnabas was kind, but the reality that a great missionary team divided over Mark had to disturb him. How would you feel if Paul—the missionary, a great leader of the church—didn't see you fit for the work, that your immaturity and lack of courage was something he couldn't allow in his ministry?

Yet now, years later, we find Paul wanting to see Mark one last time. Perhaps he wanted to let him know that he had heard about his ministry with Peter and was proud of his work. Paul forgave John Mark. He reconciled with him before winter—before it was too late.

In Our Service to Others

In another passage, Paul teaches us that we are given certain spiritual gifts for the task of ministry. "And He gave some *as* apostles, and some *as* prophets, and some *as* evangelists, and some *as* pastors and teachers, for the equipping of the saints for the work of service, to the building up of the body of Christ" (Eph. 4:11–12).

These verses explain that apostles, prophets, evangelists and pastors, who are the leaders of the church, are called to equip Christians for service and ministry. Paul further explains in First Corinthians 14 that we are all one body in Christ. Each part of the body has a function. In this sense, all of us are called to service. We all have a ministry to perform.

The apostle Paul served the Lord up to the last moments of his life. Even as he was about to die, he wanted to invest his life in the next generation by writing a letter to a young minister. We call this book Second Timothy. Are you using your gifts to serve Christ by serving others? Are you actively involved in investing your life in others?

Unless you decide *right now* that you are going to minister, you probably won't. Don't put it off. Don't waste your life.

In Expressions of Love

Another area that I would encourage you to act upon is letting those you care about know that you love them. Many have invested in your life. Your mother, father, siblings, friends, teachers, pastors or coaches may have made significant contributions to your life.

Just as Paul wanted to see Timothy one last time, is there someone in your life that you need to thank before it's too late? Is there someone who would love to hear how much you love them? Who do you need to thank?

A few years ago, I visited my parents near Athens, Georgia. One afternoon, we were at the mall browsing through a Christian bookstore. I looked through the window of the store and saw my dad talking to an elderly gentleman who looked familiar. When my dad came back into the bookstore, he asked me, "Did you recognize that fellow?" I replied, "He does look familiar." Dad said, "That's Brother Bob."

Bob was my pastor through my teenage years. I came to know Christ under his ministry. The last time I saw him, I was in his study. That's when I told him I had decided to move to another church that was closer to the university I attended. I felt led to become involved in their college ministry. I know now that he must have been disappointed. Yet he was both gracious and supportive. That was our last meaningful conversation and it had been twenty years ago.

When my dad told me who it was, I immediately knew I needed to go and speak with him. By then, he knew that I was pastoring a large church, much larger than any he had ever pastored. He was retired and had never pastored a large, influential church. Bob had even lamented to my dad that only a few young men had been called into vocational ministry under his leadership.

It made me wonder if he saw value in his ministry. I knew what I should do, yet I was somewhat nervous. I felt bad; I should have already called him. What would I say? Was it too late to encourage him? To thank him? I struggled over the next few minutes, mustering up my courage and wrestling with what I would say. When I turned to leave the store, I looked into the mall and he was gone. I looked around but I couldn't find him. I said to myself that as soon as I returned to Florida, I would give him a call. When I returned home, however, I didn't immediately make the call. A few weeks later, my dad informed me that Brother Bob had passed away. I never took the opportunity to thank him one last time for his ministry in my life. I failed to act immediately, and therefore didn't act at all.

Several years prior, a friend named Tommy came into my room at the university. I noticed a sense of reflection, almost sadness, in his voice and demeanor. This was strange since he was usually very outgoing and somewhat of a free spirit.

I asked him what was wrong. He replied that it would have been his late mother's birthday that day. He then began to share his story with me. A few years before, he had written his mom a five-page letter, thanking her for being a great mom.

Tommy admitted that he had really given his mom problems (and I believed him). Usually he would have shunned the idea of writing this type of letter, but decided one day just to do it. He poured out his heart to her. He asked her forgiveness for the problems and heartache he had caused her. He thanked her for her love, support and grace. He told her how much he loved her. He then told me that he gave her the letter and pretty much forgot about it.

Then, after his mother died, he began to rummage through her belongings. She had a box in which she saved all of her precious things. He opened the box and found his letter on top. It was worn and had obviously been read many times. He then said, "I regret many things in my life. However, the one thing I will never regret is writing that letter. I didn't realize it would mean so much to her." Tommy had been the greatest of encouragers to his mom because he did not put off what he had to do. He did it immediately.

Why Not Now?

Why do we procrastinate? Why do we put off making a commitment? Why do we ignore a call to action? The reason, I often hear from people, is that they simply lack discipline. This lack of discipline, however, usually stems from a lack of motivation.

One is that we are simply not motivated enough. For some reason, whatever God is leading us to do next doesn't seem important enough for us to do now. Perhaps we tell ourselves little stories in our head. We think that one more day will not make a difference, or that what we say or do will not impact a situation. Maybe we think that we're too busy, that someone else needs to step up this time. Perhaps our lack of motivation comes with the feeling of fatigue and overcommitment. If we are too tired or too busy to obey God, we are then saying "yes" to something that is outside of God's will.

For a good example of the repercussions of procrastination, let's look at French history.

At the beginning of his reign, Louis XV was one of the most beloved kings in France's history. When he took power in 1744, France was in horrific condition and Paris looked like it had been hit by a storm. Louis XV made promises to devote great effort and attention to restore France to prominence again. The people loved him, not so much for what he *had done* but for what they hoped he *would do*. They showed their love by giving him the name "Louis the Well-Beloved." Thirty years later, Louis XV lay sick and at the point of death. The churches didn't pray. The people didn't pray. No one prayed. In fact, Louis "The Well-Beloved" had become the most hated man in France. In 1744, Louis might have asked, "What have I done to be so loved?" However, in 1774, he might have asked, "What have I done to be so hated?" The truth is he had done nothing![3]

This contemporary Christian song by Matthew West says it well as it calls us to do something right now.

"Do Something"

I woke up this morning
Saw a world full of trouble now
Thought, how'd we ever get so far down
How's it ever gonna turn around
So I turned my eyes to Heaven
I thought, "God, why don't You do something?"
Well, I just couldn't bear the thought of
People living in poverty
Children sold into slavery
The thought disgusted me
So, I shook my fist at Heaven

Said, "God, why don't You do something?"
He said, "I did, I created you"

If not us, then who
If not me and you
Right now, it's time for us to do something
If not now, then when
Will we see an end
To all this pain
It's not enough to do nothing
It's time for us to do something

I'm so tired of talking
About how we are God's hands and feet
But it's easier to say than to be
Live like angels of apathy who tell ourselves
It's alright, "somebody else will do something"
Well, I don't know about you
But I'm sick and tired of life with no desire
I don't want a flame, I want a fire
I wanna be the one who stands up and says,
"I'm gonna do something"[4]

Courageous faith requires action. Whatever God is leading you to do, do it now!

Discussion Questions

1. What is God leading you to do right now? Bible reading? Prayer? Job hunting? Marriage counseling?
2. Is there an area of service or ministry on which you need to act?
3. What step of faith would God have you take right now?

13

Going the Distance

Aremarkable thing happened at the 1968 Olympics. While competing in the marathon in Mexico City, John Stephen Akhwari of Tanzania suffered cramps due to the high altitude of the city. At the nineteen-kilometer point, during the forty-two-kilometer race, Akhwari fell after being hit by some other runners while jockeying for position, cutting and dislocating his knee and severely wounding his shoulder as he hit the hard pavement. But Akhwari continued running and finished the race in great pain—and in last place.

When he finally crossed the finish line, a full hour after the winner, a cheer came from the small crowd that remained. When later interviewed, a reporter asked him, "Why did you continue? You were hurt. No one would have blamed you if you had quit." Akhwari replied, "My country did not send me five thousand miles to start the race. They sent me five thousand miles to finish the race."[1]

There is something admirable and special about a person who refuses to quit amidst great adversity. We admire someone who keeps getting up after falling down time and time again. All of us go through circumstances in our lives when we're tempted to quit, and the Akhwaris in life inspire us to keep going. We become tempted to give up in tough times because we feel hopeless. We think quitting would be the greatest feeling we could imagine, because it would rescue us from our stress and discouragement.

Thus far in the previous chapters, we have presented that we need to overcome our spiritual vertigo. That is, we must reconcile what we see, hear and experience with our faith. Then we can make our move toward courageous faith. However, after we move forward in courage, we also need the endurance to finish what we start. Hebrews 10:36 teaches, "For you have need of endurance, so that when you have done the will of God, you may receive what was promised."

Even when we act immediately under God's guidance, we may have to wait on the Lord to respond or intervene in our lives. Why must we wait? Well-meaning people often tell me "just wait on the Lord." Why wait? I could be serving God more if He would send the blessing now. Life is short—I don't have time to wait!

As we look at Hebrews 10–12, we conclude our study by looking at one final key point—a necessary ingredient to push through spiritual vertigo is endurance.

The book of Hebrews was originally written to Jewish Christians who were no longer lion-chasers and giant-killers. In many ways, they were experiencing spiritual vertigo. The readers were Hebrew Christians who were facing persecution. Many were compromising their faith. They were drifting back to Judaism, although staying in the church. This behavior led to several warnings in the book:

- Don't drift. "For this reason we must pay much closer attention to what we have heard, so that we do not drift away *from it*" (Heb. 2:1).
- Don't harden your heart. "Do NOT HARDEN YOUR HEARTS AS WHEN THEY PROVOKED ME, / AS IN THE DAY OF TRIAL IN THE WILDERNESS" (Heb. 3:8).
- Don't become dull of hearing. "Concerning him we have much to say, and *it is* hard to explain, since you have become dull of hearing" (5:11).
- Don't refuse the Word. "See to it that you do not refuse Him who is speaking. For if those did not escape when they refused him who warned *them* on earth, much less *will* we *escape* who turn away from Him who *warns* from heaven" (12:25).
- Don't become discouraged and quit (see 10:32 – 12:3).

The key verse in this passage is Hebrews 11:36 when the writer states that we need endurance *after* we do the will of God. Often referred to as the "Hall of Faith," Hebrews 11 is a gathering of Old Testament examples of enduring faith. Hebrews 12 concludes the argument by giving us the supreme example of Christ Himself. Why is it so dangerous to quit? What causes discouragement? How do I wait on God? If I do not endure, will I miss God's will?

The Cost of Quitting

Hebrews 10:32 exhorts us to remember: "But remember the former days, when, after being enlightened, you endured a great conflict of sufferings." This again points to the fact that enduring faith must remember the blessings of the past. Hebrews 10:35 tells us that we must have "confidence." This word is the Greek work for "public courage."[2] The writer refers to the Old Testament prophet Habakkuk (see 2:3–4) in verses 37 and 38 as a warning against cowering or retreating. The resulting thought comes through the word "destruction" in Hebrews 11:39: "But we are not of those who shrink back to destruction, but of those who have faith to the preserving of the soul."

"Destruction," comes from the same Greek word Judas used when Mary poured the perfume on Jesus' feet. He said she "wasted" it.[3] The writer of Hebrews tells us that if we do not endure and receive the blessings of God, we will waste it. We will waste our lives.

Quitting Damages Our Faith

A consequence of quitting is the damage it does to our faith. When we don't wait long enough for God to show us His grace and power, when we don't wait and receive the promise, we blame God for not coming through. In a sense, we take Him off the throne of our lives and become our own rescuer. As a result, our trust in God decreases as our trust in self often grows. Os Guinness comments on this.

> The agonizing stretches a believer on a rack. If we maintain faith, we feel tortured even more and no one seems to come to our rescue. All that is wanted, our torturer says, is that we recant and deny that anyone will come to our aid. Our faith as believers is then caught: heads-I-win, tails-you-lose. If we maintain faith, there seems to be no guarantee that our rescuer will come to our aid, and our situation is torture only because we do maintain faith. On the other hand, if we recant, we will be free and we will be our own rescuer. So, the choice is flattering. This is the way doubt reasons with

faith under the trial of waiting, and if faith gives in, its recanting is doubt.[4]

Quitting becomes habit-forming. Each time you rescue yourself, you feel a sense of relief. You relieve yourself of stress and possible failure. It's like going to work, looking the boss straight in the eye, telling him what you think of him and walking off the job. You may feel a sense of relief and satisfaction as you leave his office, like a weight lifted from your shoulders.

Then you get home and realize you now have to tell your wife and children you no longer have a source of income. Quitting becomes your escape, your temporary relief, but in no way does it solve your problem. Just as sports, pornography, television, shopping and exercise become a source of relief for some, quitting becomes a habitual escape for others. If you are not careful, you can become a "runner" habitually fleeing from the challenges in life.

I have friends in the ministry who are "runners." A few years ago, a friend called and asked me to help him find another church to pastor because his deacons and leaders were no longer following him. So he moved to another church, and eight months later, he asked me to help him find a new church because he was facing many of the same problems.

The average stay of a pastor in my denomination is four years. The point is that you are not the only one tempted to give up, to look for greener pastures, to dismount a dying horse. However, quitting oftentimes is a permanent solution to a temporary problem. As you give up, you will do serious damage to your faith. My friend could never get past the difficulties and adversities of the ministry. He began to view people as a problem rather than a ministry. Each time he quit, he found it easier to quit the next time. He never grew to believe that God is so good that He can overcome any obstacle.

Quitting Stunts Our Growth

One of the reasons for waiting is to mature us in Christ. James 1:2 teaches, "Consider it all joy, my brethren, when you encounter various trials." The result of enduring faith is that our spiritual development will be in our present stage of life.

In Romans 5:3–5, Paul states, "Not only this, but we also exult in our tribulations, knowing that tribulation brings about perseverance; and perseverance, proven character; and proven character, hope; and hope does not disappoint, because the love of God has been poured out within our hearts through the Holy Spirit who was given to us."

Paul says we can have joy in our trials because these trials bring about perseverance or endurance in our lives. These trials—coupled with perseverance—produce proven character. We prove to ourselves what God can do and what He can do through us. We become more mature in Him.

This leads to hope, which is the Old Testament idea of faith. Paul adds in Romans 5:5, "hope does not disappoint." Your maturing faith will not disappoint. You will receive the promise (see Heb. 10:36).

Quitting Robs God

When we quit, we testify to the world that God is weak. We testify that it doesn't pay to trust God. We say that following Christ is no different than not following Christ. This doesn't glorify the Lord. In fact, it has the opposite effect in the world. When we quit, we rob God of the privilege of pouring out His love toward us, blessing our lives, being our rescuer, and making us a living testimony to the world.

Suppose there are two ladies with physical issues. One says that God healed her. The other lady is not healed, but her friends and coworkers see how positively she is facing her adversity. They see the faith she has in God. They witness the joy she has in spite of her adversity. Which lady will the lost world be most impressed with?

While Christians might glory in the healing, nonbelievers may not be as impressed. Perhaps they would even doubt the healing altogether. But chances are the woman who remained faithful without getting healed would be a lasting testimony to the nonbelieving community.

Quitting Reveals Our Relationship with God

The willingness to wait reveals our relationship with others. It reveals how much we think of them or how important they are to us. For example, a businessperson calls to take you out to lunch. Let's say he wants to either sell you something or introduce you to his business. He's the one who called you, and he's the one who needs you. He is thirty minutes late for the meeting. Chances are, if you continue to wait for him, you won't be very receptive to his ideas since you don't have a deep relationship with him.

However, if your grown child is late for lunch, you're more willing to wait. You will probably be more willing to listen to your child's reason for being tardy and far more willing to get over it. Since you do not have a close relationship with the salesman, you may not even care why he is late. Our willingness to wait on God reveals our current relationship with Him. The more we love Him, the closer we feel toward Him, the more willing we are to wait.

Quitting Keeps Us from Receiving

Hebrews 10:36 explains the most tragic result to us: "For you have need of endurance, so that when you have done the will of God, you may receive what was promised." We won't be able to receive the promise or blessing from God. This promise has the idea of an agreement with God if we follow His will. The exhortation is to follow completely. If we quit halfway down the trail, we will not receive the blessing promised at the end of that agreement.

The Causes of Quitting

How We Were Raised

This can be traced, oftentimes, to how we were raised. If parents are "runners," the chances are higher that their children will be as well. Children learn more from the actions of their parents than from what they say.

Then there are "helicopter parents" who, as mentioned in chapter 3, hover over their children. They rescue their children from every point of adversity—from teachers who do not know how smart they are to the coaches who fail to realize their enormous athletic potential.

Children are persuasive and can manipulate their parents to do for them what they can do for themselves. As a result, without proper parenting, they grow up without building the muscles of character and patience. This often manifests itself in quitting school, dropping classes, leaving jobs and experiencing marital difficulties. Romans 5:3 states, "And not only this, but we also exult in our tribulations, knowing that tribulation brings about perseverance." When we allow our children to work through their trials, they build character. Part of good character is patience. When we build patience in our children, this better prepares them to endure life's difficulties.

The Stanford Marshmallow Experiment was a series of studies on delayed gratification conducted in the 1960s and '70s by psychologist Walter Mischel, then a professor at Stanford University.

In these studies, four-year-olds were given a marshmallow and told they would be rewarded with a second marshmallow if they waited until the tester returned. During the fifteen-minute wait, many of the children ate the marshmallow immediately. Others covered their eyes, kicked the desk in front of them, or even stroked the marshmallow as if it were a tiny stuffed animal.

Over six hundred children took part in the experiment. Mischel and his team found that, forty years later, the children who were able to wait for the second marshmallow tended to have better life outcomes such as better educational attainment, less drug addiction and less obesity. The gratification delayers also scored an average of 210 points higher on the SAT.[5]

The lesson is clear. If we don't teach children patience, they will learn little else. An impatient person often expresses their self-centeredness. They want instant gratification. They want God to serve them. They will even grow to resent God for His lack of cooperation. When we stop being our child's rescuer or hero and allow them to depend on Christ, they learn that God is good and they can count on Him.

Who We Trust

Another area of challenge is one we all face. We have a propensity to place other things on the throne of our lives. We may believe we trust God; but when we are pressured, when the trials come, when the blessings are delayed, our lives reveal who or what is really our Lord.

When I faced adversity, I had to fight the temptation to trust in my latest idea. I tended to think that hard work could cure anything. When I was in college, I worked my way through school by selling cemetery plots door-to-door (we were the last people to let you down). When I found myself in a slump, I just worked twice as hard until I started closing deals again. This practice has carried over to most areas of my life. When our church plateaus in attendance or ministry, I have a tendency to simply work harder.

I admit that my resources are my first thought instead of prayer. I fight as my own rescuer. I trained myself to think that most of life depends on me, though I know it's not true. I know I can do nothing without Christ. I know Jesus said, "I am the vine, you are the branches; he who abides in Me and I in him, he bears much fruit, for apart from Me you can do nothing" (John 15:5).

Yet I have to take a step back and remind myself of this each time I face a trial or setback. What trial are you facing today? What are you waiting on God for? As you wait, who are you counting on to be your rescuer?

How We See Faith

As I have said, faith stands between two worlds—the "no longer" and the "not yet." I must believe that He is and that He rewards those who seek Him (see Heb. 11:6). To build faith, we must see the past from God's perspective. We need to be thankful for all the good He has done, and then we can believe God for the future.

Where does this leave us? How can we go the distance until we receive the blessing?

The Course of Endurance

Hebrews 11 gives us great insight into enduring faith. The heart of the problem the Hebrew Christians are facing is at the core of their faith. They are drifting or cowering back because they are not convinced that God is good. They are experiencing spiritual vertigo.

The entire epistle builds toward Hebrews 11:1–12:3 in a message on enduring faith. What can we learn? How can we go the distance?

Look Behind You

Hebrews 11 tells us to remember all God has done. Since faith stands between the "no longer" and the "not yet," the author of Hebrews looks and remembers the "no longer." This is fundamental in overcoming spiritual vertigo. Remembering causes us to look at how God has blessed us and guided us through the difficulties of the past. As we are grateful for those blessings and interventions in our lives, it propels our faith into the future.

Although chapter 11 of Hebrews begins with a brief description of faith, the remainder of the chapter looks at the past, recounting the great men and women who possessed enduring faith. For example, the Bible says:

- By faith, Abel offered to God a better sacrifice (see Heb. 11:4).
- By faith, Noah built an ark (in 120 years) to save the world (see 11:7).
- By faith, Abraham obeyed God and went to a country where he had never been, looking for a city (a future city received in heaven) (see 11:8–10).
- By faith, Sarah waited ninety years before having a baby (see 11:11–12).
- By faith, Moses was hidden for three months as a baby (see 11:23).
- By faith, Moses chose to endure ill-treatment by the people of God rather than to enjoy the passing pleasures of sin (see 11:24-25).

As the writer of Hebrews finishes his exhortation for the Hebrew Christians to return to their passion for God, he challenges them to remember.

If we're going to run the distance, we must constantly remember how God has blessed us and be thankful. This is one reason reading the Bible is so important.

As we read Scripture, God speaks to us and encourages our hearts through the lives of those who went before us. We learn that Joseph waited thirteen years between the time his dream of ruling came and the time of its fulfillment. We read how Moses spent forty years on the back side of the desert (until the age of eighty) before God placed His staff in Moses' hand and made him ready to lead.

We read of Job's suffering, and the persecution and suffering of the apostle Paul. We also see the frailties of the disciples as they walk with Jesus. We witness the plights and failures of

Peter, the doubts of Thomas, the conversion of Nicodemus, the forgiving heart of Jesus with the adulterous woman, the provision of Christ as He feeds the five thousand, God's power over the evil world, and the sacrifice of Mary pouring the perfume over Jesus' feet. Then we read about the death of Christ and His hours of suffering on the cross.

God's Word says that the Scriptures were written for our encouragement. Looking at the past through God's eyes builds our faith for the future. We not only look to the past to see what God did in the lives of others, but we must constantly look at our own past blessings with gratitude.

I'm not merely referring to positive thinking, or taking lemons and making lemonade. I'm not speaking of just looking at the bright side. We are looking at the facts. God is always working in our lives to bring us closer to Him.

God has blessed you! The blessings and favor of God are all over you, and you may not see it because we tend to look at what we lack rather than what we have. I think perhaps we expect God to be that "helicopter parent." We expect God's world to revolve around us.

When our ancestors were out on the farm, there was a deep dependence on God. They prayed for rain, safety and health. They didn't have much and looked to God as their resource.

Fast forward to the twenty-first century. We are blessed with so much. We have cell phones, computers, nice cars, cable television and appliances. More people are graduating from high school than ever before. More people are getting college degrees.

Yet those things never seem to satisfy. The pursuit of more makes us more self-dependent and less God-dependent.It seems the more we have, the less grateful we are. The more we have, the more we expect to have. We credit ourselves with gathering our own resources and then we take these resources for granted. We believe we can do it ourselves. However, when the day comes that believing in yourself is not enough, where will you go?

As a believer, I must acknowledge that everything I have comes from God. I am entitled to nothing and can only cling to the cross, where every blessing is supplied. Look behind you. What are you grateful for? How has God blessed your life? Look at the evidence of His love, care and grace.

One of the things I can do to help me remember what God has done is share my faith. When I tell someone else about Christ and His cross, a part of me relives my testimony.

I recall the first time I witnessed for Christ. The leader of our youth group challenged us to share Christ with five people over the upcoming month. He gave us five survey cards and five gospel booklets called *The Four Spiritual Laws*.

I visited a couple, that first week, with whom I was very close. I was very nervous as I fumbled through the survey.

Then I asked them if I could share the booklet with them. As I talked, the booklet shook nervously in my hand. I think they saw how hard it was for me, which only caused them to take the material more seriously.

Near the end of the presentation, I remember almost coming to tears myself as I described what Jesus did for us on the cross. When I finished the booklet, I asked them if they wanted to receive Christ and they did. I was hooked!

Wow! What a spiritual experience. I felt God's presence all over that home.

Over the years, each time I shared my faith, it brought me to a special place of gratitude. I also find that people will often open up and talk about their past and their experiences. This not only gives me an opportunity to apply the gospel to their situation, but increases my gratitude quotient for how God rescued me.

Look Up

Another ingredient to enduring faith is to look up to Jesus. Hebrews 12:1–2 teaches us: "Therefore, since we have so great a cloud of witnesses surrounding us, let us also lay aside every encumbrance and the sin which so easily entangles us, and let us run with endurance the race that is set before us, fixing our eyes on Jesus, the author and perfecter of faith, who for the joy set before Him endured the cross, despising the shame, and has sat down at the right hand of the throne of God."

In order to stay encouraged during the doubtful times, we need a focal point.

> On day six of the ill-fated Apollo 13 mission, the astronauts needed to make a critical course correction. If they failed, they might never return to Earth. To conserve power, they shut down the onboard computer that steered the craft. Yet, the astronauts needed to conduct a thirty-nine-second burn of the main engines. How to steer? Astronaut Jim Lovell determined that if they could keep a fixed point in space in view through their tiny window, they could steer the craft manually. That focal point turned out to be their destination—Earth. As shown in the 1995 hit movie, *Apollo 13*, for thirty-nine agonizing seconds, Lovell focused on keeping the earth in view. By not losing sight of that reference point, the three astronauts avoided disaster.[6]

Hebrews 12:2 reminds us that to finish our life mission successfully, we must fix our eyes on Jesus, the author and perfector of our faith.

God has certainly tested me. One of my most difficult trials came when I was in college. I often played basketball during my recreation time. Our court had a rubber floor, which was good because you didn't need good shoes to keep you from slipping. It was bad too because your feet gripped the floor so well that it was easier to injure a knee or ankle.

One day, as I ran down the floor on a fast break, I cut hard around a defender, severely turned my ankle and tore every ligament in it. The swelling was so severe that it traveled up to my knee and made it impossible for me to wear a cast for three weeks. As a result, I missed class for those three weeks due to the pain and the need to keep my foot elevated. In pain and having missed so much of my senior year, I became angry.

To add insult to injury, during this time I was an interim pastor for a church about thirty miles away. After I had served about six months, they found a permanent pastor. The chairman of the deacons called me and told me the news. They also informed me that they wanted me to come back one last Sunday, preach, and let them have a going away party for me.

As I listened on the phone, I could hardly wait until he finished. After all I'd been through, I certainly was not in the mood to preach. As soon as he finished his speech, I planned to tell him "no"! I wasn't upset with him or the church. I was upset with God.

Understand a little of my story. Previously, I was a business major at a large university. After my call to ministry, I transferred to a Bible college. I lost almost two years of credits but had no regrets. However, entering my mid-twenties and in my last semester of college, I needed to plan for my future. Because of the injury, it looked doubtful that I would graduate at all.

I sat around in pain for three weeks. I had just been outfitted with my cast and crutches, and I was having big pity party. After all, I had done so much for God. As soon as the deacon finished telling me the church plans, I responded.

However, instead of saying an emphatic "no," I suddenly heard, "I would be glad to" come out of my mouth. "Where did that come from?" I thought. After I hung up the phone, I realized I couldn't say "no." Even in my anger and discouragement, somehow Jesus was still my focal point. I look back on that incident as being a turning point in my life—the day I learned I couldn't quit on God.

Look Ahead

I love Hebrews 12:3, where it says, "For consider Him who has endured such hostility by sinners against Himself, so that you will not grow weary and lose heart."

When we look to the past with thanksgiving, then to Jesus as our focal point, we realize we have a future and a hope. God has something great for you—great in His eyes and joyful in yours. However, you can't quit before the blessing comes. I love the words written years ago by Paul Simon of the music duo Simon and Garfunkel. The song title is simply, "The Boxer."

> *In the clearing stands a boxer,*
> *And a fighter by his trade*
> *And he carries the reminders*
> *Of every glove that laid him down*
> *Or cut him till he cried out*

In his anger and his shame,
"I am leaving, I am leaving."
But the fighter still remains.[7]

God did not send us here to *begin* a race—God sent us here to *finish* the race. Courageous, balanced faith finishes well.

Discussion Questions

1. Can you think of a time when you walked away from a task too soon? What could have been the results?
2. What are you discouraged about today?
3. If you wanted to quit, why do you think you would do so? An early childhood experience? A failed relationship?
4. Who are you really trusting?
5. What can you do right now to encourage yourself to stay the course? Look behind? Look above? Look ahead?

Conclusion

During my bout with physical vertigo, I needed medical help to get something my body was lacking. That ingredient was fluid. In the emergency room, the doctors placed me on an intravenous drip and by the time I left the hospital a few hours later, I felt normal again.

All of us struggle with spiritual vertigo. We too need something applied to our lives to help us overcome our doubts and fears. That ingredient is the presence of the Holy Spirit. Acts 1:8 tells us "But you will receive **power** when the Holy Spirit has come upon you; and you shall be My witnesses both in Jerusalem, and in all Judea and Samaria, and even to the remotest part of the earth." Jesus promised us in John 4:14 "But whoever drinks of the water that I will give him shall never thirst; but the water that I will give him will become in him a **well of water** springing up to eternal life."

Our spiritual power, our water of life, is God, the Holy Spirit. Do you have the Spirit in your life? He comes into our lives the moment we receive Christ as our Lord and Savior. The problem many face is the experience of spiritual vertigo even in relation to their salvation. They lack assurance of their salvation. Without salvation, we do not possess the power of the Spirit to deal with spiritual vertigo. We don't have the spiritual insight to look beyond what we see, hear or experience.

Several years ago, while attending a worship service, Pam and I heard a message on the assurance of salvation. On the way home, Pam asked if I enjoyed the message. I told her I enjoyed it but didn't feel it applied to me. After all, I had no doubts about my salvation. She shocked me when she said, "Well, I think it applied to me."

Keep in mind, my wife professed her faith as a child. I knew of no one who exemplified Christ more than Pam. After a year as a pastor's wife, at a time when I was also attending seminary, I was definitely stunned by her comment. She never before expressed her doubts.

When we arrived home, we opened the Scriptures together and I reminded her of the assurance she could experience. Then I shared a little illustration that helped her. I'll share it with you as well in just a moment.

In order to have assurance of your salvation, you must understand the foundational principles of the gospel. Begin by realizing how much God loves you. John 3:16 teaches us, "For God so loved the world, that He gave His only begotten Son, that whoever believes in Him shall not perish, but have eternal life." Realize also that God has a purpose for your life. Jeremiah 29:11 says, "'For I know the plans that I have for you,' declares the LORD, 'plans for welfare and not for calamity to give you a future and a hope.'" So why don't we experience this love and purpose?

The Bible also teaches that we're all sinners, separated from God. "For all have sinned and fall short of the glory of God" (Rom. 3:23). In my life, I have shared Christ with many people. Most people find it difficult to see that they fall short in God's eyes. Claims like, "I keep the Ten Commandments," are often used. I remember a particular young man who was very entrenched in the idea that he didn't need to be saved. I asked if he had *ever* put anything before God. He replied, "Of course I have." I said, "Yes, I have too." The first commandment says, "You shall put no other gods before Me." Like me, he had broken the first commandment many times. I asked about the second commandment: "You shall not make for yourself an idol." All of us have idols—those things that hold first place, ahead of God. He agreed he had broken that commandment as well.

As I journeyed through the Ten Commandments (honor your father and mother, you shall not steal, you shall not commit adultery—even in your mind), he realized that he had broken all Ten Commandments. If we are honest with ourselves, we'll admit that we're guilty of breaking them all as well.

Because we have all committed sin, we have become separated from God's love. That's why Jesus came to die on the cross for our sins: "But God demonstrates His own love toward us, in that while we were yet sinners, Christ died for us" (Rom. 5:8). It's further expressed: "When you were dead in your transgressions and the uncircumcision of your flesh, He made you alive together with Him, having forgiven us all our transgressions, having canceled out the certificate of debt consisting of decrees against us, which was hostile to us; and He has taken it out of the way, having nailed it to the cross"(Col. 2:13–14).

Then, the Bible teaches us to apply these truths. John 1:12 teaches, "But as many as received Him, to them He gave the right to become children of God, *even* to those who believe in His name." Is that it? Just ask Christ into your life? Nothing to work for? Nothing to do? Seems like a strange religion, doesn't it?

All a person must do is humble themselves before God, ask forgiveness for their sins, receive Christ and rely on God's grace.

Ephesians 2:8–9 tells us, "For by grace you have been saved through faith; and that not of yourselves, *it is* the gift of God; not as a result of works, so that no one may boast."

Grace lives at the very heart of the gospel. God's undeserved favor toward us is absolutely essential. We must ask Christ to do for us what we cannot do for ourselves. If I worked for my salvation, then I could boast or brag about it. Salvation would then be about what I did. I would be my own rescuer. I would thank myself for being so good. Then I would place my confidence in my own life. I could easily justify putting myself first in my life. In essence, I would become my own object of worship. But because I rely solely on God's grace, He alone is worthy of worship.

We often doubt our salvation because we believe we have some part in it, even a small one. We then wonder if we're good enough. Did Christ change our lives enough? When we're saved at a very young age, as in the case with Pam, assurance often becomes even more challenging. It's difficult to remember the changes that took place in our lives at age six.

As I mentioned, I shared a story with her that night, and I will share it with you now. There was a boy who always doubted his salvation. He went forward in church service invitations to rededicate his life.

One day, at lunch, he sat under an old oak tree in the middle of a pasture. Burdened in his heart, he bowed his head and prayed to God, "Lord, if I'm not saved, I pray one last time that you'll come into my heart." Then he took a stick, pulled out his pocketknife, and carved "Saved" and the day's date into the piece of wood. He then hammered it into the ground to "nail down his salvation."

A few weeks passed and the young boy again began to doubt. He told the devil, "Follow me." He went out into the pasture, walked up to the tree, and pointed to the piece of wood. He proclaimed, "See there? Saved! It even has the date!" The boy never doubted again.

That evening, Pam prayed one last time. She prayed that if she had never received Christ before, she would receive Him right then. She nailed down her salvation, ending her doubts.

What about you? Do you know that you have the power to overcome spiritual vertigo? Do you know, for certain, that Christ lives in your heart? You can know for sure. First John 5:13 states, "These things I have written to you who believe in the name of the Son of God, so that you may know that you have eternal life." If you're not certain that you're a Christian, I want to invite you to pray a prayer that will lead to this assurance:

"Lord, thank You for loving me. Thank You for going to the cross and dying for my sins. If I have never been saved, I pray one last time that You'll forgive me of my sins, and come into my heart. I trust that you came in because the Bible teaches, '. . . for whoever will call on the name of the Lord will be saved.'"

Did you pray that prayer? If so, let me encourage you to take this book to your pastor. Show him the prayer you prayed and ask for his help with the next steps toward courageous faith.

God bless!

Notes

Introduction

1. Timothy J. Keller, "Praying Our Doubts," Gospelinlife. com, February 20, 2000, accessed June 20, 2014, http://www.gospelinlife.com/praying-our-doubts-5240.html.
2. Thom S. Rainer and Jess W. Rainer, *The Millennials: Connecting to America's Largest Generation* (Nashville: B&H Publishing Group, 2011), 22.
3. John S. Dickerson, *The Great Evangelical Recession: 6 Factors That Will Crash the American Church . . . and How to Prepare* (Grand Rapids: Baker Books, 2013), 100.
4. Thom S. Rainer, "The Most Common Factor in Declining Churches," *ThomRainer.com* (blog), May 31, 2014, accessed July 24, 2014, http://thomrainer.com/2014/05/31/common-factor-declining-churches/.

Chapter 1

1. Mark Batterson, *In a Pit with a Lion on a Snowy Day: How to Survive and Thrive When Opportunity Roars* (Colorado Springs: Multnomah Publishers, 2006), 9-10.
2. Bob Sjogren and Gerald Robison, *Cat & Dog Theology: Rethinking Our Relationship with Our Master* (Colorado Springs: Biblica, 2003), 5.
3. Mark Rutland, "Language, Leadership and the Pursuit of Quality," *The Leader's Notebook* (blog), Global Servants, April 8, 2015, http://globalservants.org/connect/

blog/238-language-leadership-and-the-pursuit-of-quality.

4. Thomas Chan, "Uncommon Sense," *University of Minnesota. UThink: Blogs at the University Libraries,* January 26, 2012, accessed March 29, 2016, https://wayback. archive-it.org/338/20150621053110/http://blog.lib.umn. edu/meyer769/psy_1001/2012/01/uncommon-sense. html.

5. C.J. Mahaney, *Living the Cross Centered Life: Keeping the Gospel the Main Thing* (Colorado Springs: Multnomah Publishers, 2006), 13.

6. Ibid., 21.

7. Ibid.

8. Augustus M. Toplady, "Rock of Ages," 1776, accessed March 30, 2015, http://library.timelesstruths.org/music/ Rock_of_Ages/.

9. Art Buchwald, "At $772,500, Those Golf Clubs of JFK's Were a Steal," *Los Angeles Times,* May 8, 1996, accessed July 18, 2014, http://articles.latimes.com/1996-05-08/ news/ls-1557_1_golf-clubs.

10. Andy Campbell, "Elvis Presley's Bible Sells for $94,000 at Auction, but Stained Underwear Finds No Taker," Huffpost Weird News, *The Huffington Post,* September 10, 2012, accessed July 8, 2014, http://www.huffing-tonpost.com/2012/09/10/elvis-presleys-bible-auc-tion-94000-stained-underwear_n_1870575.html.

11. William Temple, *Citizen and Churchman* (London: Eyre & Spottiswoode, 1941), 74.

Chapter 2

1. J.P. Moreland and Klaus Issler, *In Search of a Confident Faith: Overcoming Barriers to Trusting in God* (Downers Grove: IVP Books, 2008), 16.

2. James Strong, *Strong's Expanded Exhaustive Concordance of the Bible* (Nashville: Thomas Nelson, 2009), s.v. "hupostasis."

3. Ibid., s.v. "pisteuo."

4. Os Guinness, *God in the Dark: The Assurance of Faith Beyond a Shadow of Doubt* (Wheaton: Crossway, 1996), 203.

5. Andy Stanley, "Heroes, Part One–X-Ray Vision" (audio message, North Point Resources, 2011), CD-ROM.

6. Guinness, *God in the Dark*, 200.

7. Stephen Eardley, "Blessings," *2003 Conference: Reconnections & New Directions* (Lester B. Pearson College, 2003), CD-ROM.

8. Timothy J. Keller, "The Lordship of Christ," Gospelinlife.com, May 14, 2004, accessed February 23, 2014, http://sermons2.redeemer.com/sermons/lordship-jesus-christ.

Chapter 3

1. Ronald Dunn, *When Heaven Is Silent: Trusting God When Life Hurts* (Fort Washington, PA: CLC Publications, 2008), 71.

2. Ibid., 72.

3. Kornelis H. Miskotte, *When the Gods Are Silent* (London: Collins, 1967), 252-3.

4. J.P. Moreland and Klaus Issler, *In Search of a Confident Faith: Overcoming Barriers to Trusting in God* (Downers Grove: IVP Books, 2008), 45.

5. Roy Hession, *The Calvary Road* (Fort Washington, PA: CLC Publications, 2014), 23.

6. Charles Stanley, "Brokenness" (FBC Atlanta, 1997), CD-ROM.

7. A.W. Tozer, *The Root of the Righteous* (Camp Hill, PA: WingSpread Publishers, 2006), 77.

8. F.B. Huey, Jr., *The New American Commentary, vol. 16, Jeremiah, Lamentations* (Nashville: Broadman Press, 1993), 174.

9. Howard G. Hendricks, *The Battle of the Gods* (Chicago: Moody, 1972), 8.

Chapter 4

1. Henry T. Blackaby, Richard Blackaby, and Claude V. King, *Experiencing God: Knowing and Doing the Will of God* (Nashville: Broadman & Holman Publishers, 2008), 32.

2. Moreland and Issler, *In Search of a Confident Faith*, 64.

3. Strong, *Strong's Concordance*, s.v. "proginosko."

4. Arnold Fine, "Letter in the Wallet," *Reader's Digest* (Brooklyn, NY: Jewish Press, 1984), 49.

5. Dunn, *When Heaven Is Silent*, 29.

Chapter 5

1. Andrew Delbanco, *The Death of Satan: How Americans Have Lost the Sense of Evil* (New York: Noonday Press, 1996), 3-4.

2. Ted Tally, "The Silence of the Lambs," The Internet
    Movie Script Database, accessed February 10, 2014,
    http://www.imsdb.com/scripts/Silence-of-the-Lambs.
    html

3. Matthew N.O. Sadiku, *Choosing the Best: Living for What
    Really Matters* (Bloomington, IN: AuthorHouse, 2012),
    136.

4. Ibid.

5. Stephen R. Miller, *The New American Commentary*, vol.
    18, *Daniel* (Nashville: B & H Publishing Group, 1994),
    284.

6. Strong, *Strong's Concordance*, s.v. "agnosia."

7. David E. Garland, *The New American Commentary*, vol.
    29, *2 Corinthians* (Nashville: B & H Publishing Group,
    1999), 210-12.

8. Chuck Colson, interview by Larry King, "Chuck Colson
    Live with Larry King," *BreakPoint Online*, January 6,
    1993, accessed February 22, 2014, http://www.break-
    point.org/multimedia/entry/18/14883.

9. A.W. Tozer, *I Talk Back to the Devil: The Fighting Fervor
    of the Victorious Christian* (Camp Hill, PA: WingSpread
    Publishers, 2008), 12-3.

10. Strong, *Strong's Concordance*, s.v. "methodeia."

11. Ibid., s.v. "pale."

12. Ibid., s.v. "diabolos."

13. Seth Godin, *All Marketers Are Liars: The Power of Telling
    Authentic Stories in a Low-Trust World*, repr. ed. (New
    York: Portfolio, 2009), 2-3.

14. Shaun Groves, "The World, the Flesh & the
    Devil, Part 4: The Devil," *Shaun Groves* (blog),

June 6, 2013, http://shaungroves.com/2013/06/
the-world-the-flesh-the-devil-part-4-the-devil/.

15. Rose Publishing, *Armor of God Wall Chart – Laminated*,
accessed March 3, 2016, http://www.rose-publishing.
com/Armor-Of-God-Wall-Chart-Laminated-P69.
aspx#.VtipiuZcBdw, wall chart.

16. John MacArthur, *Ephesians: Our Immeasurable Blessings in
Christ*, MacArthur Bible Study Guide Series (Nashville:
Thomas Nelson, 2006), 338.

17. F.F. Bruce, *The Epistles to the Colossians, to Philemon, and
to the Ephesians*, The New International Commentary
on the New Testament (Grand Rapids: W.B. Eerdmans,
1984), 407.

Chapter 6

1. Luis Lugo et al., *U.S. Religious Landscape Survey—Religious Beliefs and Practices: Diverse and Politically Relevant*
(Pew Forum on Religion & Public Life, June 2008),
accessed February 21, 2014, http:www.pewforum.org/
files/2008/06/report2-religious-landscape-study-full.pdf.

2. Matt Slick, "Manuscript Evidence for Superior New Testament Reliability," Christian Apologetics & Research
Ministry, accessed February 22, 2014, https://carm.org/
manuscript-evidence.

3. Strong, *Strong's Concordance*, s.v. "theopneustos."

4. William M. Ramsay, *The Bearing of Recent Discovery
on the Trustworthiness of the New Testament* (London:
Hodder & Stoughton, 1915), 222.

5. Nelson Glueck, *Rivers in the Desert: A History of the
Negev, Being an Illustrated Account of Discoveries in a*

Frontierland of Civilization (New York: Farrar, Straus & Cudahy, 1959), 136.

6. Frank Harber, *Beyond a Reasonable Doubt: Convincing Evidence for Christianity* (Lynchburg, VA.: Liberty House, 1996), 93.

7. Ibid., 91.

8. Matt Slick, "The Disciples Stole Jesus' Body and Faked His Resurrection," Christian Apologetics & Research Ministry, accessed February 22, 2014, https://carm.org/disciples-stole-jesus-body-and-faked-his-resurrection.

9. Ken Curtis, "Whatever Happened to the Twelve Apostles?" Christianity.com, accessed February 23, 2014, http://www.christianity.com/church/church-history/timeline/1-300/whatever-happened-to-the-twelve-apostles-11629558.html.

10. Lionel Luckhoo, *The Question Answered: Did Jesus Rise from the Dead?* Luckhoo booklets, back page, quoted in "The Case for Christ," All About the Journey, accessed March 1, 2016, http://www.allaboutthejourney.org/the-case-for-christ.htm.

11. Timothy J. Keller, "The Meaning of the City," Gospelinlife.com, October 5, 2003, http://sermons2.redeemer.com/sermons/meaning-city.

12. Glenn Kirby, "The Soar of Man" (sermon, West Hills, CA, April 16, 2006).

13. Bill Ricketts, "Letter from Darla" (sermon, Campus Crusade for Christ from University of Georgia, Athens, GA, October 1974).

Chapter 7

1. Andy Stanley, "Heroes, Part Two–Expect the Unexpected" (audio message, North Point Resources, 2011), CD-ROM.
2. Raymond Angelo Belliotti, *Jesus the Radical: The Parables and Modern Morality* (Lanham, MD: Lexington Books, 2013), 2.
3. Ralph Howe, "I've Got Rhythm," Ralph Howe Ministries, accessed March 3, 2016, http://www.ralphhoweministries.com/iaeve-got-rhythm/.

Chapter 8

1. Henry Ford, quoted in "7 Must Read Success Lessons from Henry Ford," Mr. Self Development, accessed February 24, 2014, http://www.mrselfdevelopment.com/2010/06/7-must-read-success-lessons-from-henry-ford/.
2. Benjamin Disraeli, quoted in "Famous & Not So Famous Quotes," RFQK.COM, accessed February 24, 2014, http://rfqk.com/secret-of-success.html.
3. John F. Kennedy, "John F. Kennedy Address at Rice University on the Space Effort" (speech, Rice University, Houston, TX, September 12, 1962), accessed February 27, 2014, http://explore.rice.edu/explore/kennedy_address.asp.

Chapter 9

1. *Braveheart*, directed by Mel Gibson (1995; Hollywood CA: Paramount Pictures, 2000), DVD.
2. "Israel's Exodus from Egypt and Entry into Canaan," Jesus Reigns, July 13, 2009, accessed March 8, 2016,

https://jesusreigns.wordpress.com/2009/07/13/israels-exodus-from-egypt-and-entry-into-canaan/#more-6115, map 2.

3. Andy Stanley, *The Best Question Ever: A Revolutionary Approach to Decision Making* (Sisters, OR: Multnomah Books, 2004), 32.

4. Rainer and Rainer, *The Millennials*, 6-7.

5. Ronnie Floyd, *Our Last Great Hope: Awakening the Great Commission* (Nashville: Thomas Nelson, 2011), 128.

Chapter 10

1. Jim Henry, "Sin—The Defeat of Faith," sermonsearch, accessed June 28, 2014, http://www.sermonsearch.com/sermon-outlines/13331/sin-the-defeat-of-faith/.

2. *The Expositor's Bible Commentary with the New International Version*, ed. Frank E. Gaebelein, vol. 3, *Deuteronomy, Joshua, Judges, Ruth, 1 & 2 Samuel* (Grand Rapids: Zondervan, 1992), 284.

3. Timothy J. Keller, *Counterfeit Gods: The Empty Promises of Money, Sex, and Power, and the Only Hope That Matters* (New York: Dutton, 2009), xiv.

4. David M. Howard, Jr., *The New American Commentary*, vol. 5, Joshua (Nashville: Broadman & Holman Publishers, 1998), 197.

5. Ronald Dunn, "The Sin of Achan," Ron Dunn, accessed July 2, 2014, http://rondunn.com/the-sin-of-achan/.

6. Stephen Olford, "Interview on Preaching Workshop," in *Reaching All: 172*, Pine Avenue Baptist Church, 1974, cassette.

7. Timothy J. Keller, "Elijah and the Voice," Gospelinlife. com, October 13, 1996, accessed July 2, 2014, http:// www.gospelinlife.com/elijah-and-the-voice-5922.html.

Chapter 11

1. Strong, *Strong's Concordance*, s.v. "doxazo."
2. John Piper, *Don't Waste Your Life* (Wheaton: Crossway Books, 2003), 32-3.
3. *Merriam-Webster OnLine*, s.v. "risk," accessed July 2, 2014, http://www.merriam-webster.com/dictionary/risk.
4. "Pakistani Christian Woman Appeals Over Death Sentence," *BBC News*, November 12, 2010, accessed February 1, 2014, http://www.bbc.com/news/ world-south-asia-11745100.
5. Batterson, *In a Pit with a Lion*, 89.
6. C.S. Lewis, T*he Chronicles of Narnia: The Lion, the Witch and the Wardrobe* (New York: Harper Trophy, 1994), 86.
7. Alister McGrath, "The Religious Symbolism Behind the Chronicles of Narnia," *BBC Religion & Ethics*, November 21, 2013, accessed February 1, 2014, http://www.bbc. co.uk/religion/0/24865379.
8. Batterson, *In a Pit with a Lion*, 79.

Chapter 12

1. Francis P. Martin, *The Kingdom's Economy: A Guide to Proper Giving* (Mustang, OK: Tate Publishing & Enterprises LLC, 2011), 129.
2. Ronald Dunn, "Three Plus One," Ron Dunn, accessed July 2, 2014, http://rondunn.com/three-plus-one/.

3. George Graham, "Ye Did It Not," *Expositor and Current Anecdotes*, vol. 16 (Oxford: Lightning Source UK, 2012), 431-2.

4. Matthew West, vocal performance of "Do Something," by Matthew West, on *Into the Light*, Sparrow Records, 2012, compact disc.

Chapter 13

1. John C. Maxwell, *The Success Journey: The Process of Living Your Dreams* (Nashville: Thomas Nelson, 1997), 155-6.

2. Strong, *Strong's Concordance*, s.v. "parrhesia."

3. Ibid., s.v. "apoleia."

4. Guinness, *God in the Dark*, 210.

5. Walter Mischel, "Deferred Gratification–The Stanford Marshmallow Experiment," What Is Psychology?, accessed April 4, 2016, http://www.whatispsychology.biz/deferred-gratification-stanford-marshmallow-experiment.

6. Lou Nicholes, "39 Second Correction Saves Astronauts," Family Times (sermon illustration), accessed February 28, 2015, http://www.family-times.net/illustration/Correction/201204/.

7. Simon and Garfunkel, vocal performance of "The Boxer," by Paul Simon, on *Bridge Over Troubled Water*, Columbia Records, 1970, compact disc.

PUBLICATIONS

Fort Washington, PA 19034

This book is published by CLC Publications, an outreach of CLC
Ministries International. The purpose of CLC is to make evangelical
Christian literature available to all nations so that people may come
to faith and maturity in the Lord Jesus Christ. We hope this book has
been life changing and has enriched your walk with God through the
work of the Holy Spirit. If you would like to know more about CLC,
we invite you to visit our website:

www.clcusa.org

To know more about the remarkable story of the founding of
CLC International we encourage you to read

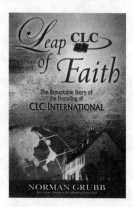

LEAP OF FAITH

Norman Grubb

Paperback
Size 5¹/₄ x 8, Pages 248
ISBN: 978-0-87508-650-7
ISBN (*e-book*): 978-1-61958-055-8